Herne the Hunter
of
Windsor Forest

ERIC L. FITCH

GREEN MAGIC

Green Magic
53 Brooks Road
Street
Somerset
BA16 0PP
England
www.greenmagicpublishing.com

Designed and typeset by Carrigboy, Wells, UK
www.carrigboy.co.uk

ISBN 978 1 915580 21 4

GREEN MAGIC

Contents

Foreword

This book is a thoroughly revised, expanded, and revamped edition of my 1994 book, *In Search of Herne the Hunter*. Since then, I have amassed a wealth of new material that was not in the earlier book, and have widened the scope of topics covered. The main criticism of the original book was its lack of references, so I have corrected this oversight. In recent decades Herne has become well-known, especially in the Neo-Pagan world and the media. He is said to haunt Windsor Great Park wearing antlers upon his head and presaging national disaster. But to the wider public, he is known from Shakespeare's reference to him in *The Merry Wives of Windsor*, and from W. Harrison Ainsworth's 1843 novel, *Windsor Castle*.

Ainsworth's work features Herne, who in one scene is described thus: "... a weird figure, mounted on a steed as weird looking as himself, galloping through the trees with extraordinary swiftness. This ghostly rider wore the antlered helmet described by the Earl of Surrey, and seemed to be habited in a garb of deer skins. Before him flew a large owl, and a couple of great black dogs ran beside him." Herne also carried a hunting horn which, when he put it to his lips, issued forth bright blue flames and thick smoke, and he was sometimes accompanied by snakes and "a swarm of horribly grotesque, swart objects, looking like imps." A vivid picture indeed.

Although there is romantic embellishment here, Ainsworth's retelling is probably based on earlier tradition. However, in order to get at the roots of Herne's story, as well as the sources, I am going to base much of the discussion in this volume on Ainsworth's novel. Although his telling of the tale is regarded largely as fiction, it contains so many mythical themes which have much in common with earlier folklore and mythology. These themes, I believe, are so well interwoven into the legend that it is too much of a coincidence that they should all appear in one story. Whether Ainsworth was borrowing from local oral lore, or whether he penned the story himself using themes he knew through his studies, is not known. So this volume explores the supernatural and the misty past, as well as the historic and literary backgrounds to the legend of Herne, with the new title of *Herne the Hunter of Windsor Forest*.

NOTE

I was brought up in Windsor, so I was aware of Herne from an early age. Also with Slough nearby, I would go to the town now and again over the years. This leads me to belatedly thank Slough Library for arranging an exhibition on Herne the Hunter sometime around the late 1980s, which motivated me to write my first book on the subject.

The Merry Wives of Windsor

BY WILLIAM SHAKESPEARE

William Shakespeare
(Martin Droeshout, 1623)

The earliest mention of Herne the Hunter (and the only historic record) is to be found in William Shakespeare's play, which was first performed on St George's Day, 23rd April, 1597, at the Feast of the Order of the Garter in the presence of Queen Elizabeth I. It was in Vicars' Hall behind St George's Chapel in Windsor, being commissioned by the Queen to coincide with the making of her cousin, Lord Hunsdon, a Knight of the Garter. As to its publication, this took place in 1602. The play introduced Herne the Hunter to Britain, and ultimately to the rest of the world, in his guise as an otherworldly figure.

But first, here is the well-known passage from the play which began the interest in Herne, appearing in Act 4, Scene 4, and spoken by Mistress Page:

> *"There is an old tale goes that Herne the hunter,*
> *Sometime a keeper here in Windsor forest,*
> *Doth all the winter-time, at still midnight,*
> *Walk round about an oak, with great ragg'd horns;*
> *And there he blasts the tree and takes the cattle*
> *And makes milch-kine[1] yield blood and shakes a chain*
> *In a most hideous and dreadful manner:*
> *You have heard of such a spirit, and well you know*
> *The superstitious idle-headed eld[2]*
> *Received and did deliver to our age*
> *This tale of Herne the hunter for a truth."*

This quote is the most authentic reference to Herne, despite its brevity, and all subsequent versions represent either romantic embellishments of Shakespeare, oral tradition handed down over generations, or a combination of both. Incidentally, Shakespeare was not pleased with the play, and it seems that he had written it in a hurry. And now a brief summary of the work which is comical and full of intrigues.

The play begins with Sir John Falstaff, an impoverished knight, taking a liking to two women, Mistress Page and Mistress Ford – both quite well off and already married. Falstaff, a dishonest, lazy and lecherous old man, is probably the favourite of Shakespeare's comic characters. He tries to seduce the two married women and sends identical letters to the two ladies expressing his love for them, in the hope of defrauding them of some of their money, and at the same time having affairs with both. He attempts to

---

1   Milch-kine in the modern vernacular translates as "milk cows" – "milch" obviously meaning milk, and "kine" an archaic word for the plural of "cows". The latter derives from the Anglo-Saxon *cyna*, the singular being *cu*.
2   "eld" is an archaic word meaning "the past" or "olden times".

procure the help of his two servants, Nym and Pistol. They refuse, and so he sacks them, but they immediately rush off to let the ladies' husbands know of Falstaff's plan, and they make up their minds to trick him. The wives fool Falstaff on two occasions. The first culminates in him ending up in a dirty river; and the second, after disguising himself as a witch, he is set upon and beaten. Mistress Ford finally tells her husband of Falstaff's ruse, and both married couples get together to play a ruse on Falstaff himself.

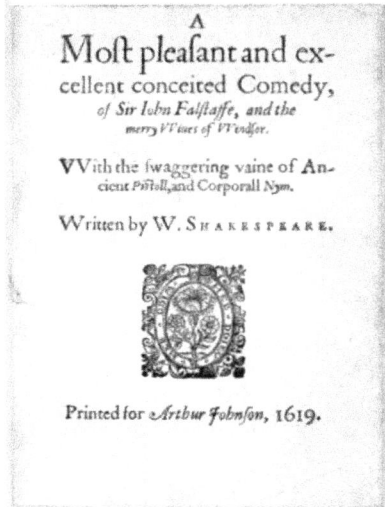

A

Moſt pleaſant and ex-
cellent conceited Comedy,
*of Sir Iohn Falſtaffe, and the
merry VViues of VVindſor.*

VVith the ſwaggering vaine of Ancient *Piſtoll,* and Corporall *Nym.*

Written by W. SHAKESPEARE.

Printed for *Arthur Iohnſon,* 1619.

The women manage to persuade Falstaff to disguise himself as Herne the Hunter, complete with antlers on his head, and to meet up with them near Herne's Oak at night in Windsor Forest, with Falstaff hoping for an assignation. However, the two wives along with their husbands, friends, children dressed as fairies, and Mistress Quickly dressed as Queen of the Fairies, in order to taunt and scare him. Mistress Quickly, an inn-keeper, prepares the fairies with this instruction:

> *"But till 'tis one o'clock*
> *Our dance of custom round about the oak*
> *Of Herne the Hunter, let us not forget."*

Mistress Page encourages everyone as follows:

> *"Let them from forth a sawpit rush at once*
> *With some diffused song; upon their sight*

We two in great amazedness will fly:
Then let them all encircle him about
And fairy-like, to pinch the unclean knight,
And ask him why, that hour of fairy revel,
In their so sacred paths he dares to tread
in shape profane."

To which Mistress Ford adds:

"And till he tell the truth,
Let the supposed fairies pinch him sound
And burn him with their tapers."

And Falstaff appears to be quite willing to impersonate Herne, as he states in Act 5:

"Divide me like a bribe-buck, each a haunch;
I will keep my sides to myself, my shoulders for the
fellow of this walk,
and my horns I bequeath your husbands,
Am I a woodman? ha! speak I like Herne
the hunter?"

Falstaff is terrified by these figures who surround him, pinching and burning him with their candles. They eventually reveal themselves. The play ends with everybody laughing at the antics they had all got up to, and at Falstaff's humiliation, with the two women turning out to have the upper hand. However, Falstaff is forgiven and even invited to the wedding of Mistress Page's daughter Anne and her beau.

It could be that Falstaff's punishment was influenced by a folk custom of "skimmington rides" which took place in southern England at the time. In the cases where a husband or wife had been found to be unfaithful or having committed harm on the other, then he or she would be dragged from their home and made to ride back-to-back through the village on a donkey. In Devon, it became a mock hunt, whereby the wrong-doer was dressed as a stag and chased by huntsmen on horses and boys disguised as dogs. It has also been suggested that Falstaff's punishment could have been influenced by the Greek myth of Actaeon. This hero was walking through a forest when he came across the goddess Artemis bathing naked in a lake, who caught him spying on her. Straightaway she turned him into a deer and set his own hunting dogs on him, which attacked and ripped him to shreds. But as Petry points out that: "the play contains numerous references to people, places, things, and even topical events well-known in the Windsor area," that Herne, his Oak and legend are specific to Windsor, and so it is highly likely that the Classical Actaeon myth has no connection with Falstaff's comeuppance.[3]

Falstaff at Herne's Oak, Act V Scene V with Mistresses Page and Ford
(Michele Beneditti, 1793, Wikimedia Commons)

---

3   Petry, pp13–14.

A pirate edition of the play appeared, but with a poor text, with the following version of the Herne legend:

"Oft you heard since Horne the Hunter dyed,
That women to affright their little children,
Ses that he walkes in shape of a great stag.
Now for that Falstaffe hath bene so deceived,
As that he dares not venture to the house,
Weele send him word to meet us in the field,
Disguised like Horne, with huge horns on his head,
The houreshalbe just betweene twelve and one,
And at that time we will meet him both:
Then would I have you present there at hand,
With little boyes disguised and dressed like Fayries,
For to affright fat Falstaffe in the woods."

Although the first edition of the play was published in 1602, this pirate version came out in the same year, with the twelve lines above revealing a different telling of Herne and Falstaff. Note that Herne here becomes Horne. The play was also adapted in a revised version by John Dennis in 1702, titled *The Comical Gallant*. Apparently Queen Elizabeth had seen *Henry IV Parts I and 2*, and was so taken with the character of Falstaff in these plays, that she requested Shakespeare to write another play featuring him in love, resulting in his writing *The Merry Wives of Windsor*.

Shakespeare seems to be aware of folklore in general, but first some background to begin with. In Shakespeare's day, folklore played an important part of everyday life, when such figures as fairies, goblins and elves were believed in. Witches as well were considered to be real, and in *Macbeth* the well-known three witches play a part; and in *A Midsummer Night's Dream* fairies make many appearances. The quote from the latter work includes the following:

"… that shrewd and knavish sprite
Call'd Robin Goodfellow: are not you he
That frights the maidens of the villagery;
Skim milk, and sometimes labour in the quern
And bootless make the breathless housewife churn,
And sometimes make the drink to bear no barm,
Mislead night-wanderers laughing at their harm?
Those that Hobgoblin call you and sweet Puck,
You do their work, and they shall have good luck."

So, folkloric themes would have been familiar to audiences of his plays, and it is not surprising that Shakespeare used local folklore as well as references to real Windsor people and events in the play. Anne Page, for instance, is recorded to have been buried at Windsor Parish Church in 1617, at a cost of two shillings, paid for by the parish council. Also, the names used in the play are those used locally in the Windsor area, such as Herne, Page, and Ford. In addition, towns not far from Windsor are mentioned, including Datchet, Eton, Old Windsor, Colnbrook, Maidenhead and Reading. It is possible, therefore, that the playwright could not have invented the legend of Herne the Hunter any more than he would have done for the inhabitants and goings-on at Windsor. It is recorded that he spent some time in Windsor gathering material for the play. He stayed at a local hostelry, but there are three contenders for which inn it actually was.

One was called *The Bottle on the Moore* which was situated at Frogmore in the Great Park (which changed its name to The Hope Inn, and is no longer extant); and another went by the name of The Harte & Garter Hotel which is still in existence, situated in Thames Street opposite the castle. This now possesses commemorative stained glass windows on the staircase featuring characters from the play, such as Falstaff, Mistress Page, Mistress Ford, Mistress Quickly and Bardolph. However, this was previously two inns: The White Hart and The Garter Inn.

Weather Vane, Harte and Garter Hotel (Brian Robert Marshall, Wikimedia Commons)

The latter hostelry is referred to a number of times during the play, and it could well have been where the playwright lodged whilst working on the play for fourteen days. The inn was the place where Falstaff and his followers stayed for £10 per week. The rich Eton-educated Richard Gallys was the manager of The Garter Inn and Mayor of Windsor for five terms, as well as becoming an MP in 1562. It is possible that Shakespeare based his character of the inn-keeper in the play on him. As to where Shakespeare carried out his research for the play, it could well have been in The King's Head in Church Street close to the castle.

In the play, one of Herne's attributes is that he "makes milch-kine yield blood," or in modern terms "causes cattle to produce blood instead of milk." It was considered that as cows have their offspring about April/May time, this could be connected with the traditional custom of placing honeysuckle and rowan sprigs in cow sheds on 2nd May, in order to protect the cattle from coming to any harm from witches. Also it was thought that the milk produced is in this way is up to standard and a good yield. Rowan is well-known to have been used to prevent the evil deeds of witches; and honeysuckle was also seen as a powerful protective agent. However, either these remedies were not used in Windsor or Herne was impervious to them.

I should add that the public house *The Merry Wives of Windsor* in St Leonard's Road, Windsor, is now *The Windsor Grill* restaurant – another drinking establishment and a traditional name gone. It was once one of the oldest Windsor pub names, but its character has been maintained, even though there are obviously alterations. The seventeenth century timber-framed building is Grade II listed, and the public house frontage was constructed around 1900.

The Merry Wives of Windsor public house, now
The Windsor Grill (whatpub.com)

Works Consulted

Herne the Hunter: A Berkshire Legend, by Michael John Petry (1972). https://www.windsor.gov.uk/ideas-and-inspiration/blog-late

Windsor Forest

"LONG shalt thou flourish, Windsor! bodying forth
Chivalric times, and long shall live around
Thy Castle the old oaks of British birth,
Whose gnarléd roots, tenacious and profound,
As with a lion's talons grasp the ground."
– Thomas Campbell

BERKSHIRE

Before the arrival of the Romans, the area of Berkshire was part of the Celtic tribal region of the Atrebates. Upon the arrival of the Saxons, the earliest reference to the county of Berkshire comes from the pen of the Welsh monk Asser (later Bishop of Sherborne) in his *Life of King Alfred* dating from 893, where he refers to Alfred being born in Wantage in Berkshire. He also mentions that its name is derived from *Berroc wood*, "where box[1] grows in great abundance." *Berroc* comes from the Celtic word *barro* denoting a summit, indicating a local hill, the chalk mound on which Windsor Castle stands; and the name for the surrounding forest was taken from this. Come the Anglo-Saxons, they named the area *Bearu-ac-scire* or "Grove-Oak-Shire", the county later coming under the rule of Wessex. The eastern boundary of the county is marked by Old Windsor, the village where the Saxon kings held court before moving to (New) Windsor with the coming of the Normans. But the fifteenth century English chronicler John Brompton stated that "Berkshire

---

1 Box is a slow-growing, evergreen tree. Its wood was used to make musical instruments. It also had many medicinal properties, such as curing gout, skin problems, epilepsy, headaches, leprosy and rheumatism.

derives its name from a certain bare oak in the forest of Windsor, at which the people of the area were wont to congregate." However, this derivation is doubtful.

In 1889, the emblems of the oak and stag were adopted for the new Berkshire County Council, and when the county was granted its own coat of arms in 1947, it incorporated them into its design as well. It has been thought by many over the centuries that the oak referred to Herne's Oak, and that the stag related to Herne himself, but whatever their origins, they go back into the mists of time, perhaps deriving from a pagan stag cult and tree worship.

In 1957, Queen Elizabeth II granted royal status to the county, thus giving us *The Royal County of Berkshire*. In 2017, the flag of Berkshire was registered with the Flag Institute. It features an oak tree and a stag that has antlers with twelve tines – a characteristic of a royal red deer stag. The two symbols denote the county forestry and its herds of deer.

The Berkshire Flag (Wikimedia Commons)

WINDSOR

The place-name "Windsor" itself seems to derive from the Saxon words *windels* and *ora* denoting a "river bank with a windlass[2] or winch," changing into *Windelsora* by the eleventh century. So,

---

2 A windlass is a contraption enabling carts to be hauled up the bank of a river, in this case the Thames at Old Windsor.

in modern English, it could be phrased as "landing place with a windlass."

The town in which Windsor Castle is situated is technically New Windsor, as the village of Old Windsor (two and a half miles downstream on the Thames) was originally known as just Windsor. Its position was close to the Thames for transport, and the medieval manor house placed conveniently as a popular hunting lodge. Here the Saxon kings held court before the Normans arrived and built Windsor Castle upstream on Castle Hill. Runnymede is close by, where King John signed Magna Carta (or Great Charter) in 1215. Ainsworth's 1843 novel *Windsor Castle* placed his legend of Herne the Hunter in the reign of Richard II, but it seems that he never actually lived at the castle at all.

ROYAL WINDSOR FOREST

To begin with, by the sixth century CE, Windsor Forest consisted of a minor Romano-British settlement, which survived longer than other areas of southern England by about 100 years, when the Anglo-Saxons eventually brought it under their control. This may explain why themes such as someone hanging from a tree and the Wild Hunt led by Woden (Odin) were mixed with earlier Celtic legends (see chapters *A Windsor Legend* and *The Wild Hunt*).

Windsor Great Park now consists of 5,000 acres (2,020 hectares), although centuries ago it was far larger (when it was just known as Windsor Forest), and traditionally it was the private hunting ground of Windsor Castle. It is also the only royal park managed by the Crown Estate rather than by The Royal Parks.

Edward III instigated some of Windsor Forest as a deer park in 1368, and the area was extended over the centuries until, under George II, the park contained about 1,300 red deer. However, in 1785, George III had the deer removed, but in 1806 the park still contained around 300, so this seems to be contradictory. King James I was especially fond of the chase, and was very pleased on becoming king to find that Windsor Forest was well stocked with deer. It was said that when a stag had been felled, he would quickly cut its throat, rip open its belly, after which he would wallow in its blood, which he would then commence to daub over his fellow hunters.

It appears that during times of war, forests were cut down at an alarming rate, but there were some new plantations made. One of the earliest recorded was in Windsor Forest in 1580, when some thirteen acres were sown with acorns – and by 1625, the area had grown into a wood of tall young oaks. It had been necessary to fence the woodland off early on to prevent damage caused by deer and cattle. A report from the *Windsor Express* newspaper of 9th November, 1838, gives a vivid description of a hunt when Queen Victoria's staghounds were led a merry chase by an old stag which was so well-known he had been named St George (see chapter *Stags and Antlers* for more on deer in the Park).

Nowadays, the area of Windsor Great Park is a Site of Special Scientific Interest (SSSI), consisting of about 5,000 acres located south of Windsor town. It is classed as a Royal Park, which includes a deer park, and its woodland contains a large number of ancient trees and areas of parkland. The SSSI acknowledges the diversity of its invertebrates, including the violet click beetle, which makes it of international importance for these particular insects. There also exists a great variety of fungi, with a number that are exceedingly rare.[3]

Windsor Great Park has a number of sites that are worth noting, including The Savill Garden, Virginia Water (with its Roman columns from North Africa), The Valley Gardens, The Long Walk and Deer Park, Smith's Lawn, Queen Anne's Ride and Stag Meadow – all administered by the Crown Estate.

Following on from the passing of his father, Prince Philip, Duke of Edinburgh, King Charles III was appointed Ranger of Windsor Great Park in November 2022.

3 Wikipedia

A Windsor Legend

Herne the Hunter (George Cruikshank c.1843)

The legend of Herne the Hunter was originated by the author W. Harrison Ainsworth (1805–1882). He was trained as a lawyer, but gave this up and became a historical novelist. His first work, *Sir John Chiverton*, was published in 1826. Other novels included *The Tower of London* (1840), *Guy Fawkes* (1841), *The Lancashire Witches* (1849), *The Flitch of Bacon* (1854), *The Lord Mayor of London* (1862), *Tower Hill* (1871), *Merry England* (1874), *Beau Nash* (1879), and many others. But it is *Windsor Castle: An Historical Romance* (1843) that provides us with the most well-known account of Herne. The novel is a romance which includes elements of a gothic nature, portraying the pursuit of Anne Boleyn by King Henry VIII – a tale that includes Herne the Hunter, who is interweaved into the storyline. The initial publication sold over 30,000 copies, and it remained in print until the 1960s, being translated into many different languages.

It is known that Ainsworth was aware of folklore, which is revealed in a book by Thomas Keightley, titled *The Fairy Mythology Volume I*, published by Ainsworth himself in 1828. This tome covered fairy tales of the world, especially those from Europe, which were inspired by the fairy tales and mythology of the Brothers Grimm. His novels have been criticised for mingling fact and fiction, an example being *The Lancashire Witches* (1849), which distorted the account of the 1612 witch trials, turning it into a gothic novel; and nowadays Ainsworth is largely forgotten, with the possible exception of *Windsor Castle*. Ainsworth was a successful author of the nineteenth century, writing novels, essays, poetry, journalism and such short horror stories as *The Spectre Bride* and *The Sea Spirit*. He counted Dickens, Thackeray, Mary Shelley, Walter Scott and Coleridge in his circle, and had artists such as George Cruickshank illustrating his books. *Windsor Castle* was first published in instalments in *Ainsworth's Magazine* in 1842–1843. As well as appearing in the novel as a character, the legend of Herne is recounted in the chapter named Book The Fourth, Section VI, titled *The Legend of Herne the Hunter*. The novel was also adapted into a play titled *Herne the Hunter* but I have not been able to find anything further on this.

The main theme concerns Henry VIII's efforts to replace his wife Catherine of Aragon with Anne Boleyn, but Thomas Wyat and Cardinal Wolsey both have their eyes on Anne as well. The figure of Herne the Hunter, the spirit of Windsor Forest, is intertwined with the events at the castle, represented as an evil force who gathers the souls of individuals. Henry endeavours to thwart him, but in vain. The novel concludes with Anne being executed, enabling Henry to wed Jane Seymour.

However, I shall paraphrase the account of Herne's legend as told by the author. The story begins at Windsor Castle where there is a gathering, when the conversation turns to Herne the Hunter, and a character named Hector Cutbeard volunteers to relate the legend, as follows.

THE HERNE LEGEND BY AINSWORTH

W.H. Ainsworth
(Daniel Maclise, 1834)

Around the middle of King Richard II's reign (1367–1399), one of the keepers of the forest was a young man named Herne, who was a cut above the other keepers in the matters of woodcraft, which led to the King favouring him. Whenever he was residing at the castle, the King, who enjoyed hunting, was always accompanied by Herne. However, this made the other keepers jealous of him, and they plotted to find a way of getting at him, but every time they tried, they failed, and this only made Herne's position more advantageous than injurious.

Richard II (Thomas Pennant, 1726–1798)

One day, whilst the King was out hunting with his followers, they came across a hart with a huge set of antlers, which they pursued for many miles. By this time, all those following the King had ceased to keep up with him, leaving only Herne able to. The hart eventually came to a halt after having been driven to desperation, and it caused the King's horse to rear up and throw the King off his mount. If things happened in just another instant, the King would have received the goring antlers, had not Herne hurled himself between the hart and the King, receiving the blow himself. Though badly wounded, Herne managed to raise himself up a little, and plunged his knife into the animal's throat.

With the King now able to stand up again, he asked Herne what he could do for him, to recompense him for his bravery. Herne replied that he would only require a grave from the King, as his time will shortly be up. However, the King offered the attention of his best doctor, and added that, if he recovered, he would become Head Keeper with an annual wage of twenty gold coins a year. But if he died, the King would spend the annual wage in masses for his soul. Herne humbly thanked him, accepting the latter offer as it seemed to him that he would not survive, then he blew his horn and collapsed.

The King rode off seeking help, blowing on his own horn, and was soon joined by a number of keepers and others and rode to the place where Herne and the hart lay. The keepers were secretly very pleased at finding Herne in such a predicament, but they pretended to be concerned about Herne. Then the Chief Keeper, a dour old man named Osmond Crooke, began to pull out his hunting knife, stating that the best thing was to put Herne out of his misery. The King exclaimed "What! Kill the man who saved my life?!" adding that he would reward well any person who could heal him.

At this, a tall, swarthy man in strange clothes and mounted on a black horse of a wild appearance, suddenly jumped down from his steed and walked up to the King. He then spoke in a strident voice that he would accept the King's offer and would cure Herne. When the King asked him who he was, the stranger replied that he was a forester, but he was trained somewhat in surgery and healing. The King replied that he wouldn't be surprised if he was also trained in woodcraft, as well as hunting the royal deer. Crooke added that he looked like a man who was once outlawed for stealing deer, to which the stranger replied that he was no outlaw, and his name was Philip Urswick. He went on to say that he lived on Bagshot Heath, where he had joined the King's hunt, but Crooke claimed that he had not seen him, nor had the other keepers. Urswick replied that there was no keeper who could be compared as this brave hunter, and he reiterated his ability to cure Herne, if the King could reward him adequately. The King responded that if he was true to his word, he would not only be amply rewarded, but he would also be pardoned for any offence he had committed.

"Enough," replied Urswick, and taking his hunting knife he cut off the hart's head close to where the neck joins the skull, and said that it must be bound onto Herne's head. Although the keepers were astounded at this strange suggestion, the King ordered it to be carried out. So, the bleeding skull was fastened to the head of Herne with leather thongs. Urswick turned to the King, saying that Herne would be cured in a month's time, while he himself would keep watch over him until he was brought back to health. He added that he required the keepers to carry him to his hut, the King commanding them to do Urswick's bidding. A litter was made with branches of a tree (an oak?), and Herne was carried by the keepers to Urswick's small hut which was situated in the wildest region of Bagshot Heath. Here Herne's body was placed on a bed made of dried fern.

After this was completed, Crooke spoke up again, saying that Urswick would now have to earn the King's pardon, to which Urswick replied that he knew that Crooke would lose his post as Chief Keeper if Herne succeeded. At this, Crooke snarled that he wished that the deer had killed Herne outright, which was echoed by the rest of the keepers. Urswick then said that it was obvious that all the keepers intensely hated Herne, and went on to ask them what they would give him for their revenge. Crooke replied that they had next to nothing to give, to which Urswick replied that if they swore to grant his first request that he made of them, he would carry this out, to which they promptly agreed. Urswick then proceeded to state that Herne would definitely recover, but he would lose all his expertise as an archer and all his skill as a hunter. And the keepers, secretly displeased with this, went away.

A month passed and Herne, looking pale and thin, and accompanied by Urswick, had an audience with the King, who gave Herne a purse of gold coins, together with a silver horn. Herne was then appointed as Chief Keeper, and the King hung a golden chain round his neck, and ordered him to take lodgings in the castle.

About a week later, Herne regained his strength and rode with the King on a hunt, but his horse jerked and threw him, and getting on his feet he was feeling badly shaken, with the keepers eyeing one another askance. A little time later, a stag was suddenly seen by the hunters and, although Herne was riding along on a swift-footed horse given to him by the King, he ended up last in the hunt. The King came up to him, laughingly saying that he was out of practice, but all Herne could say in reply was that he could not understand what the matter with him was. The King decided to give him another chance, but everything Herne attempted went awry, so the King let him rest for a week, informing him that at the end of the period, if he did not come up to scratch, he would have to fire him, which pleased the keepers no end.

Then Herne decided not to return to the castle, but headed off wildly into the forest, where he stayed up till the evening, when he returned with a dreadful appearance. This consisted of a rusty chain hanging from his left arm which he had grabbed from a gibbet, and with Urswick's antlered skull bound to his head. He appeared to have gone quite deranged, which caused the keepers to burst out laughing, and with the wildest demeanour he rode off amongst the trees of the Home Park. An hour later, a pedlar from Datchet discovered him hanging from an oak tree, which became known as Herne's Oak. The pedlar ran to the castle to report what he had found but upon returning the body was gone, pleasing the keepers who now thought their revenge had been carried out. A search was carried out, to no avail, and when the King was alerted to this event, he was very distraught. He would have liked to have had a church service for Herne's soul, but the priests would not perform this, as he had taken his own life, which meant that the Church could not approve such a service. That night, a terrific thunderstorm occurred, and lightning struck the oak upon which Herne had hanged himself.

Of course, Crooke regained his post as Chief Keeper, but he lost his woodcraft skills like Herne, and subsequent Chief Keepers who were appointed, as well as all the other keepers, also fell under the same spell. They decided to visit Urswick to ask for his help, but he informed them that there was only one way they could break the spell. This entailed returning to the oak where Herne hanged himself, and there they would learn what to do. So they arrived at the oak at midnight. They could only just make out the tree in the darkness, but suddenly a blue flame appeared, which flitted round the tree three times and then stopped, its light falling on a figure clothed in wild garments with a chain on its left arm and an antlered skull on its head. This was Herne, and while the keepers fell down before him, he let out a fearsome laugh. The spirit of Herne then darted round the tree, rattling his chain and uttering appalling imprecations. He then bade them to come prepared for a hunt the next night, and suddenly disappeared.

The keepers, full of dread, decided to consult Urswick, who told them to obey Herne's instructions, bringing with them the black horse that the King had given to Herne, as well as the two black hounds. Again at midnight they arrived at the tree, only to see Herne stalking round the tree and hear his frightful spells. He ordered Crooke to bring the horse to him, whereupon he mounted the steed and cried out, "to the forest!" and off he went with the keepers following. Eventually, they arrived at a huge beech tree, where Herne dismounted and said some mystical words, and made bizzare gestures. Then, all of a sudden, Urswick appeared in a fiery flash, and welcomed Herne, and turning to the keepers he stated that the time had arrived for them to fulfill their promise, ordering them to form a band for Herne and accept him as leader. If they did not carry this out, he would leave them to the King's justice. Afterwards, Urswick disappeared in a flash of fire.

For many nights they performed their ghostly chase, and once the King had returned to the castle and heard of it, he wished to see it for himself. At midnight one night, the King, with many guards, joined the keepers as they rode to the oak. Here they saw Herne on the black horse, and the King asked him why he disturbed the peaceful night-time with his band. Herne replied that he wished for vengeance on Crooke and his followers. But the King demanded to know if Herne had died by his own hand, to which Herne replied that he had done so, but was driven to it by a spell laid upon him by the wretched keepers. He added that if the King would hang them on the oak, he would no longer trouble the forest whilst the King lived, at which the King said they must all die as Herne had spoken. At this, Herne vanished in a flash of fire.

The King kept his word and had Crooke and his comrades hanged on Herne's Oak, after which Herne was never seen again during the reign of King Richard II. However, the legend goes that he reappeared with a new band of keepers when Henry IV took the throne (1399), but the band was destroyed and Herne continued on, managing to evade capture for as long as Windsor Forest endures.

Ainsworth placed his legend of Herne in the reign of Richard II, who was only the age of ten when he took the throne, with regents ruling on his behalf until he was of age. He earned a reputation after his death, largely due to Shakespeare who wrote his play *Richard II* in about 1595, where the playwright portrayed him as a bad ruler. However, modern research tends to the notion that he had a personality disorder, which got worse as his reign began to end, and he was ousted by Henry Bolingbroke (in fact Henry IV – probably the first monarch to make an address in English).

The novel *Windsor Castle* itself is based around events concerning Henry VIII, who wishes to divorce Catherine of Aragon and marry Anne Boleyn, which is opposed by Thomas Wyat who wishes to wed Anne himself. Another is Cardinal Wolsey, who tries to turn Henry's attention away from Anne to his daughter, Mabel Lyndwood. Finally, Wolsey brings the matter to court, revealing Wyat's desires, almost resulting in him being executed, but Wolsey himself is ordered out of the court and he is executed. Mable and Thomas are captured by Herne, which ends up with the couple falling for each other, but as they try to escape, Mabel drowns. Meanwhile, Catherine realises that her marriage with Henry will soon be over, she warns Anne that Henry would treat her in exactly the way that she was in her marriage. After they are wed, it is revealed that Anne is involved with another, which gives Henry the evidence he needs to have her executed, the story ending with Henry's marriage to Jane Seymour.

During all this, the phantom Herne is intertwined with the plot, and Henry has to deal with the Windsor Forest spirit, a devilish influence who looks to obtain the souls of various folk, and Henry tries to stop Herne from these activities, but he fails. In the most nightmarish episode, during a thunder storm at the castle, Henry encounters Herne who, "dilated against the flaming sky, the proportions of the demon seemed gigantic. His right hand was stretched forth towards the King, and in his left he held a rusty chain." Henry asks what Herne wants, and the reply was to keep company with him, saying, "This is a night when only you and I should be abroad. We know how to enjoy it. We like the music of the loud thunder, and the dance of the blithe lightning."

Henry cries: "Avaunt, fiend! I will hold no converse with thee. Back to thy native hell!" Herne replies that Henry has no power over him, saying that his thoughts are evil, and he is about to commit a terrible deed. He goes on to say that before he committs every great crime, he will always appear to him, and that his last appearance will be before the King's end. He then laughs, adding that Henry will be drunk with the blood of his wives, and that he will have a fearful end, saying: "Thou shall linger out a living death – a mass of breathing corruption shalt thou become – and when dead, the very hounds with which thou huntedst me shall lick thy blood!" After this tirade, a dazzling brilliant flash of lightning shoots past Henry and he stands there for a few moments, almost blinded. When he can see again, the spirit of Herne has vanished. Thus this is how Herne appears in the novel – a demonic fiend.

The biographer of Ainsworth, Stephen Carver, has the viewpoint that Herne depicted in the novel is the author's best of his gothic texts, with Herne stealing all the scenes in which he is present, similarly to the way he steals souls so easily.[1] And in 1911, Stewart M. Ellis felt that the historical element of the novel was so well interwoven with the supernatural that it was very difficult to find where the everyday content ended and the occult began.

Now, as with many folk tales, there are a number of variations of the story, so here below are those of Herne.

VARIATION ONE

In this version of Herne's legend, albeit brief, Samuel Ireland (1744–1800) published his two-volume work, titled *Picturesque Views on the River Thames* (1792), which included the following account based in the reign of Queen Elizabeth I:

> "That having committed some great offence, for which he feared to lose his situation and fall into disgrace, he was induced to hang himself on this tree [Herne's Oak]. The credulity of the times easily worked on the minds of the ignorant to suppose that his ghost should haunt the spot. This rendered it a fit scene of action for the purpose of our bard [Shakespeare] to terrify and expose the cowardice of the fat knight [Falstaff], who confirms the idea of Herne's ghost being supposed to walk near this place, and is even desirous of imitating the keeper's voice, as described above."

---

1 *The Work of W.H. Ainsworth*, by Stephen Carver (2020).

VARIATION TWO

A simple local variation records that Herne was wounded by a stag which he eventually managed to kill, whereupon he became mad, tied a set of antlers to his head and then hanged himself from what became known as Herne's Oak (see *Herne's Oak* chapter). Another omits the stag altogether and puts the suicide down to his disgrace, after committing some criminal deed. Others attribute this disgrace to hunting without permission, resulting in his betrayal to the King. After hanging himself, his ghost, in the form of a stag, was said to haunt the oak, butt the trunk and tear at the roots whilst breathing fire and smoke. Two further accounts place the events in the reign of Henry VIII. The first states that his suicide was due to his being suspected of witchcraft, and that after his death his ghost was renowned for appearing to sentries at the castle (see *Encounters* chapter).

VARIATION THREE

A further version has it that Richard Herne, the King's hunter, lost his hunting skills having been gored by a fearsome stag in Windsor Forest. He then consulted a witch or wise woman, who promptly tied antlers onto his head and told him to keep them on his head for one week. But after a few days had passed, he felt that his powers had been restored and, taking his bow and arrow, he made his way into the forest so that he could ensure that he was fit enough to resume hunting. Having hit a deer with one shot, Herne was best pleased, but when he tried to remove the antlers from his head, he discovered that they had grown into his head. It was then that he recalled the witch's instruction to not to recommence hunting until he took the antlers off. The desperate Herne then hanged himself from what became known as Herne's Oak.

VARIATION FOUR

Herne was huntsman for Richard II, and one day, whilst in the Great Park, a huge stag attacked the King, threatening to gore him. Herne leapt in the stag's path and saved the King's life, but he himself was badly injured. Suddenly, a wizard named Philip Urswick appeared out of a beech tree, who told the King to attach the dead stag's antlers to Herne's head. Herne was then tied to the beech tree and survived, resulting in the King making him the head huntsman. However, the park workers became jealous and struck a deal with Urswick and framed Herne for poaching. Herne became so ashamed that he hanged himself from his oak, but his spirit was restless. The treacherous huntsmen were later impelled by Urswick to ride with Herne through the park for eternity.

VARIATION FIVE

Ainsworth added a variation at the end of his tale spoken by "a tall dark man in an archer's garb," who pointed out that the account was "wrong on many material points." He began by saying that it was true that Herne was a keeper in the reign of Richard II, that he was a master of woodcraft, and that he was favoured by the King. However he was besotted by a lovely damsel and not by a "weird forester" (Urswick?). He then abducted a nun and lived with her in a forest cave, where he brought together his fellow keepers, treating them with the King's venison and wine. Apparently the nun was the spitting image of the damsel and acute enough to bring down Herne, as it was her machinations that enabled "the fiend" to tempt him. The charms that proved his undoing were fatal to the nun as well, for in a fit of jealousy he murdered her. It was the remorse that he felt that led Herne to commit suicide. Cutbeard replied that the story may well be the true one, but it does not account for Herne's antlers. And the discussion ended there.

Herne the Hunter with Abducted Nun (George Cruikshank)

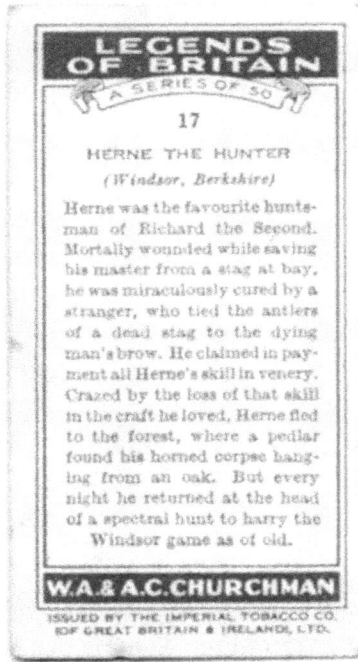

Churchman's Cigarette Cards from the 1930s

Other reasons why Herne hanged himself include such accounts as:

- he had defiled the King's ward.
- he was caught illegally hunting.
- he was suspected to have engaged in witchcraft or black magic.
- wounded by the stag, he tore off its antlers and holding them aloft he ran through Windsor Forest naked.
- for centuries his ghost would accost the castle guards who would give the alarm when he appeared.

PHILIP URSWICK

Now to the figure of Philip Urswick and his possible origins. The folklorist and mythologist, Lewis Spence, saw Herne and his healer, Urswick, to represent the rivalry between the spirit of a beech tree and that of an oak. In Ainsworth, Urswick resides in a beech tree, from which he appears in flames, which Spence saw as the "lightning spirit who animates the tree." He surmised that the name Urswick could be a corruption of Okuthor, another name for the Viking Thor, "the god who drives the thunder-chariot", but this author feels that this is probably a step too far in conjectural supposition.[2] However, Urswick certainly cuts a strange, almost shamanic figure, especially with his healing skills.

Where did this name come from? My research has led me to a former Dean of Windsor, Christopher Urswick (1448–1522), who took up his post of Canon of Windsor in 1490, becoming Dean in 1495. During this period, he oversaw the rebuilding of the Windsor Deanery and the redevlopment of St George's Chapel, and there is still an Urswick Chantry in the north west of that building. A stone screen with an inscription requesting prayers for Urswick is still extant, but now it is in the south aisle. The Albert Chapel contains a window depicting eminent figures connected with St George's Chapel, in which Urswick is included,

---

2 *The Minor Traditions of British Mythology*, by Lewis Spence (1948), pp157–158.

and on the roof his coat of arms is featured several times. In 1492, he became Registrar of the Order of the Garter. He was a close friend of Henry VII, and was a very pious and humble man, refusing the higher posts within the Church. On the inscription on his chapel screen, the last words ended as follows:

> *"O God, who by thy only begotten Son didst redeem mankind, being incarnate of the Virgin's womb and having suffered death, deliver we beseech thee the souls of Henry VII and Christopher, and all those whom Christopher offended during life, from eternal death, and bring them to eternal life. Amen. God have mercy."*[3]

Perhaps the humility and piety of Christopher Urswick struck a chord with Shakespeare, which may have morphed into the healing aspect of Philip Urswick. In fact, Ainsworth mentions the Urswick Chapel in *Book The Third – The History of the Castle*, chapter IV, amongst a list of other chapels within St George's Chapel. When he came to write the *Legend of Herne* later in the novel, perhaps he had remembered this name unconciously. As to the name Philip, the only connection with Urswick is the derivation of his first name – that it comes from the Greek name Philippos, *philos* meaning "loving", and *hippos* meaning "horse", thus giving us "horse-loving". The legend, of course, has Urswick appearing mounted on a "black, wild-looking steed."

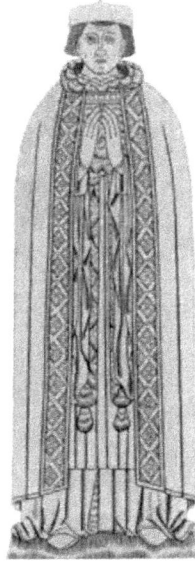

Christopher Urswick (National Archives, UK)

Could Christopher Urswick have been the inspiration for the figure of Philip Urswick? Naturally, the latter does not appear in print until Ainsworth's novel, published in 1843, but it may be

3 *The Romance of St George's Chapel, Windsor Castle,* by Harry W. Blackburne and Maurice F. Bond (4th revised edition, 1956), p23.

the case that his name could have easily been recorded in folklore, as was Herne's. The historical Urswick died in 1522, *The Merry Wives of Windsor* was written in 1597, and Shakespeare's play *Richard III* from 1592 included Urswick as a minor character in one small scene where he acts as envoy between the Earl of Derby and the exiled Earl of Richmond, the future King Henry VII.

Urswick was obviously known to Shakespeare, and the playwright incorporated local folklore into *The Merry Wives of Windsor*. Ainsworth also was well versed in folklore, and it may be that he picked up the name from the locality of Windsor, as did Shakespeare before him. Perhaps Urswick had some kind of reputation, which became part of Windsor lore.

Reviews of Ainsworth's book were mixed, with some deriding it as not being a worthy work of literature, and others who thought it was one of his most fascinating novels. In 1911, S.M. Ellis thought that he had "most skilfully, too, adapted and revivified for the purposes of his woodland romance the ancient and weirdly picturesque legend of Herne the Hunter … the whole interwoven with supernatural events in the most natural manner, so much so that it is difficult to say where the mundane ends and the occult begins." In 2003, the author Stephen Carver praised it, saying that the novel's depiction of Herne "is Ainsworth at his gothic best, rivalling Lewis, Maturin and even Byron. Herne effortlessly steals every scene in which he appears, much as he steals souls."

Origins

HERNE'S NAME

With the pure form of Herne, place-names occur in Kent and Hampshire, deriving from the Old English word "hyrne" meaning a corner or angle. But the Herne found in Bedfordshire originates from the Saxon "harum", the dative plural of "haer" meaning a stone. A similar derivation is that of Cerne Abbas in Dorset which also means stone or rock, but, in this instance, it derives from the Celtic "cairn" denoting a heap of stones. It is appropriate here to note that Cerne Abbas also has its legendary figure, the huge ithyphallic chalk giant on the hillside above the village (which has now been dated roughly to late Saxon times).

However, it is "hyrne" which seems to be the most promising, the corner or angle normally referring to a bend in a river. The Thames at Windsor, where it flows past Frogmore, does indeed make a wide bend on its way to Old Windsor, but it is unlikely to be the origin of Herne's name, as there is no mention of the Thames in his legend. It could well be connected with the Saxon word "horn" meaning a horn-like hill, as in Horne in Surrey, although Horne in Rutland derives from the Saxon "horna", indicating again a corner or bend. This aspect of curvature in both derivations seems to be the key with the Herne of legend, as it is the curved nature of his antlers which is of importance.

Now we come to the most important Herne connection, in the form of the Celtic god Cernunnos. As can be seen, it begins with the core "Cern", and the special relevance of this lies in the fact that the god was the horned god, who was often depicted with antlers (this is discussed further in the chapter *Pagan Portals*). In addition, it is of interest that the name of Cornwall in both its English form and its Cornish version, Kernow, also contains this element which refers to the corner, curved shape or horn-like aspect of the principality itself. So here we see that Horn – Herne – Cernunnos – Kernow are all aspects of the one theme of the curved horn. Herne's name is also associated with the Saxon god Woden (who was also known as Herian) who led the Wild Hunt just like Herne, and this is further dealt with in *The Wild Hunt* chapter.

FOLK ORIGINS

Thirty years have gone by since my book *In Search of Herne the Hunter* was published, and much research on such matters has led to a change in ideas of pagan survivals, spearheaded by the authors Ronald Hutton and Jeremy Harte. The chief theme that has been debunked was that of Lady Raglan's 1939 article "The Green Man" published in the journal *Folklore*, which influenced many people in the decades to come. She researched the foliated faces carved in churches and cathedrals up and down the country, and she called them the Green Man, influenced by J.G. Frazer's *The Golden Bough* which included the notion that certain folkloric ideas such as the Green Man and similar concepts were carried down the centuries.

These were then transferred to the development of folk customs like Jack-in-the-Green and the activities surrounding May Day celebrations, which then influenced the origins of customs like Morris dancing, maypole dancing, mummers' plays and the like. The Green Man was seen by Raglan as medieval carvings which had developed from ancient pagan times, representing symbols of fertility. This theme was taken on by the New Age movement, and it also became part of Neo-Pagan beliefs. This way of thinking was to spread during the 1960s and 70s, with the influence of such films as the BBC's *Robin Redbreast* (1970) and *The Wicker Man* (1973) helping things along. But the idea that folk customs have roots in the pagan past is not tenable amongst serious folklore scholars, who agree that there is no evidence at all that this is the case. And I must admit that the same goes for almost all so-called "pagan origin" figures and activities, which I have largely omitted from this current tome.

That folk customs with a "pagan" nature were once enacted are to be found in early churchmen's pronouncements. Such instances on this theme include Augustine of Canterbury (died 604) who preached a sermon which encouraged folk to severely punish those who took part in the despicable practice of dressing up like a stag or horse. Another example concerns the scholar Aldhelm (c.639–709), Abbot of Malmesbury and future Bishop of Sherborne, who is said to have been appalled in horror at revellers clothing themselves in animal costumes, especially those dressed as stags. Around the same time, Theodore, Archbishop of Canterbury (668–690), condemned those who went about garbed as beasts, clothed in animal skins and the putting on the heads of animals on the Kalends of January.[1] Particularly he complained about those dressed as stags, as well as old women (?!), which he considered devilish, and deserved a penalty of three years' penance. But as described above, there were no more reports of such folk customs after the seventh century, so it seems that the Church had succeeded in outlawing them. But as the decades passed, it became obvious that there were no actual "trails" to these activities' "pagan" beginnings, with the earliest dates being recorded around the seventeenth century and most much later.

However, there is one folk custom that just might have ancient roots, and that is the Abbots Bromley Horn Dance. The Staffordshire village of Abbots Bromley still enacts a traditional dance incorporating not only time-honoured figures and costumes, but also antlers – a feature of the Herne story.

---

1 Originally, the Kalends of January was a New Year Roman festival, but the participation in the pagan rites were still popular up until the early Middle Ages.

Although first recorded in 1686, a hobby horse was mentioned in the village in 1532, which might have been part of the event. One suggestion was that it commemorated the restoration of lost forest rights during the reign of Henry III, but this has now been dismissed. The six dancers are known as the Deer Men, who enact the dance accompanied by a musician playing a melodeon, with the tune played known as *Wheelwright Robinson's Tune*. Accompanying the Deer Men are a Hobby Horse, Fool, Robin Hood, a male Maid Marian, a boy carrying a bow and arrow and another beating time with a triangle, both boys dressed in red velvet tunics and hats.

The six Deer Men are dressed in green tunics with brown spotted sleeves and blue trousers with brown spots. The dance takes place annually on Wakes Monday – the Monday following the first Sunday after the 4th September.[2] The folklorist, Christina Hole, considered the dance to be "a ritual reproduction of a hunt, and since the purpose of hunting dances was to bring success to the hunters by imitative magic, the quarry in such performances always represented an animal known to the people, and one which they might reasonably expect to capture in their own district."[3]

There are three sets of reindeer antlers painted white with brown tips, and three painted brown with gold tips, all attached to skulls fixed to poles about fifteen inches long. These are held by the dancers as they perform their dance, carrying the skulls' antlers close to their chests, thus enabling them to be raised above the dancers' heads. The first dance takes place near the church, followed by the market place and other places in the parish, such as local pubs and farms. The dance consists of the two sets of three facing one another and dancing towards each other and back again several times, almost locking horns in the process. After this, they form into single file and then into a circle, and at the climax they are chased by the boy pretending to shoot them

2 Wakes Monday is a feast of dedication to the parish church.
3 Hole. pp8–10.

with arrows. Whilst the dancing is going on, Maid Marian pounds a small stick into a ladle in time to the music, an act which has overtly sexual overtones, providing a link with sexuality, fertility and antlers.

The Players in the Abbots Bromley Horn Dance *c.* 1900 (Wikimedia Commons)

By dusk, the dancers have covered many miles, and the weight of antlers must have taken their toll on the dancers, weighing between about 16 to 25 pounds, but they obviously think it worthwhile. The antlers (which are those of reindeer) are then returned to the local St Nicholas Church, where they are kept when not in use. In 1976, a small piece of one of the antlers was radiocarbon dated to the eleventh century, but as reindeer had been extinct in England by then, it indicates that they could only have been imported from one of the Nordic countries, which makes one wonder why, and by whom, this was carried out.

Therefore, it could be argued that the Abbots Bromley antlers could have been used for ritual and traditional purposes for centuries, with the reindeer antlers being replaced when needed. As mentioned in the chapter *Stags and Antlers*, the antler became a symbol of fertility and growth, and the Horn Dance could well have been an autumnal fertility rite. All in all, antlers obviously had deep significance over the centuries, or millennia, and it could be seen that the antlers worn by Herne are an example of such esteem. Herne the Hunter, this fusion of man and stag, may have been part of a lost folk custom long ago in Windsor, which included a man dressed as a stag who appeared, perhaps, at the winter solstice to enact the story of the defeat of winter by spring in some form of mummers' play or dance. As mentioned above, my previous Herne book went into some detail on folk customs, which have now been accepted that they were not based on ancient pre-Christian origins at all.

Summing up; even though I feel that the only custom that might (and I mean *only might*) have remote origins, is the Abbots Bromley Horn Dance. And as for Herne and his antlers – who knows? (But see also *Pagan Portals* chapter)

Boston, St Botolph's Church: Green Man Carving
(by Michael Garlick, 2016. Wikimedia Commons)

Works Consulted

The Quest for Merlin, by Nikolai Tolstoy (Hamish Hamilton, February, 1985).

Staffordshire Vicarage & Abbots Bromley Horn Dance, by John Hine (Centurion Press, 1991).

English Custom and Usage, by Christina Hole (Batsford, 3rd edition, 1950).

Herne's Oak

"Why, yet there want not many, that do fear
In deep of night to walk by this Herne's oak."
                                        – The Merry Wives of Windsor

OAK TREES

Trees feature in much world mythology, perhaps none more so than the Norse Yggdrasil, the World Ash. This tree acted as a pivot upon which the heavens revolved, and gnawing its roots was the Cosmic Serpent, Jormungand. Perched at its top was the World Eagle, Vedrfolnir, and browsing amongst its branches was the stag, Eikthymi. It was the tree upon which the god Odin (Woden) hanged himself, which is a key myth in connection with Herne and his origins. The concept of the World Tree or Tree of Life was widespread, and from very early on it was linked with the death of a saviour, normally a god who then achieved immortality. This was especially so in Palestine, where the worship of sacred trees and pillars was common before the arrival of the Israelites, such trees being of religious importance to the Canaanite goddess, Astarte. The Tree of Life is a key factor in Hebrew Cabalistic tradition, and illustrates the underlying unity within the universe. It acts as a model connecting the universe with God and humankind, and the tree's branches spread throughout creation reconciling the individual leaves and branches, which represent universal phenomena, with the unified oneness of the whole.

The most common native British oak is Quercus robur, and it is one of 300 types found in the temperate regions of the northern hemisphere. When the first settled communities in Britain emerged about 7,000 years BP, much of the country was covered in thick oak forest. The tree was therefore very familiar to the Neolithic farmers who cleared large areas of woodland by slashing and burning. However, the oak survived to become a special tree to our forebears, and this is evidenced by the many place-names which incorporate the word "oak". Examples include Oake in Somerset, Oakhanger in Hampshire (oak slope), Okeford in Dorset (oak ford), Acklam in Yorkshire (oak wood), and Accrington in Lancashire (village where acorns grew). Britain has many special oaks, including Major Oak in Sherwood Forest; Charles' Oak in Boscobel Wood, Shropshire; Augustine's Oak on the Isle of Thanet; Turpin's Oak in Barnet; and King's Oak in Windsor Great Park, which is said to have sheltered William the Conqueror. The Carmarthen Oak, popularly associated with Merlin, gave rise to the couplet:

"When Merlin's Oak shall tumble down,
Then shall fall Carmarthen town."

And it is also of interest to point out that King Arthur's Round Table in Winchester's Great Hall, dating from the mid to late thirteenth century, was cut from a single transverse section of an oak, measuring 18 feet in diameter and weighing about 185 stones. Bearing the names of a number of Arthurian knights, it was likely to have been made for Round Table tournaments. The paintwork dates from the reign of Henry VIII.

The wood of the oak is renowned for its strength, durability and elasticity, and for these reasons was much used in British shipbuilding before the age of iron. It is said that during the eighteenth century, Admiral Vernon would traverse the countryside with his pockets loaded with acorns. He apparently planted them wherever he could so that there would always be a supply of oak wood with which to build more ships. In 1827, London Bridge was demolished to make way for a new one, and in the foundations were discovered some oak piles which were as sound as when they had been installed six or seven hundred years earlier. The oldest oak tree in Britain is thought to be one found on the Blenheim Estate, which was featured in David Attenborough's 2023 TV series *Wild Isles*, and which is estimated to be 1,045 years old. This takes us to Anglo-Saxon England in 978 – 88 years before the Norman Conquest.

Oak trees have acquired a special reverence in British history and folklore. The tree was sacred to the Anglo-Saxons, who held it so because it was rarely struck by lightning. Their runic symbol for the letter "A" is ᚪ meaning ac or oak. Runes were considered to have divine or magical properties. Indeed, the Germanic peoples often looked upon the oak as being at the centre of their religious and social life. A charter dating back to 955 concerning land in Abingdon mentions a "foul oak", and there is a record of a "Woden's Oak" close to Chieveley – both historically in Berkshire, which could point to the possibility of their having once been an oak-cult in the county. Many English surnames such as Oak and

Nokes can be traced back to the tree, notably one man named Thomas del Oke recorded to be living in Berkshire in 1275.

Many villages had what was called a Gospel Oak, so called as the Gospels were read out under the tree during the annual beating of the bounds tradition on Ascension Day. At the foot of Glastonbury Tor stand two ancient oaks named Gog and Magog, referring to the male and female giants who were said to have once walked the tracks of Britain (Gog burned down a while ago). Oaks represent strength and durability, the Druids especially revering the tree in their rituals. Oak leaves were depicted on the old sixpence and shilling coins, thus acknowledging the oak's almost magical properties.

The oak was venerated by virtually all ancient European peoples, and was sacred to the various thunder gods, such as the Greek Zeus, the Roman Jupiter, the Celtic Taranis, and the Germanic Thor. In ancient Greece there were a number of oracles, the best-known being that at Delphi; however, the oldest one was the oracle at Dodona, which possessed a huge, sacred oak in which Zeus was said to be seated. Questions were put to the oracle, and the answers came from the rustling and whispering sound of the oak's leaves, which the priests interpreted, hearing voices in the leaves' rustlings. As well as this, bronze objects were hung from the oak's branches which made sounds when the wind was blowing, perhaps sounding like wind chimes. In keeping with its association with a thunder god, it was said that thunderstorms would rage at Dodona more frequently than anywhere else in Europe. The sight of a great oak struck by lightning is quite striking, and it is therefore understandable that the ancients saw the oak as a channel whereby the thunder god would communicate to humankind, with the oak tree being named the Thunder-Tree.

The Germanic tribes were renowned for their holy groves, and Tacitus refers to them in his *Germania*. The old German laws exacted a terrible punishment for those who committed the crime of peeling the bark of a tree. The offender's punishment was to have his navel cut out and nailed to the damaged part of the tree, after which he was made to walk round and round the tree until his intestines had wrapped themselves around the trunk. Thus living tissue replaced the wound the perpetrator had inflicted – a life for a life. The Prussians remained unconverted for many years after the rest of Germany, and sixteenth century writers make reference to sacrifices still being made in sacred groves. Vestiges of such practices may also have lingered late in Britain, for in 1538 a priest accompanied by an oaken idol were both burned at the stake at Smithfield in London.

The Greeks and Romans saw the acorn as the glans of the penis and thus regarded the oak as a fertility symbol. Reinforcing this was the respect shown to mistletoe growing on oak trees, the juice of which was regarded as seminal fluid, with Pliny the Elder recommending that women who wished to conceive should carry a sprig of mistletoe around on their person. The use of mistletoe at the Christmas celebrations no doubt reflects this ancient veneration, but its pagan and sexual overtones never allowed it to be accepted within the Church's festivities, as were holly and ivy. Of course, the idea of the Druid (which is derived from the Celtic word "derwydd" meaning oak-seer) dressed in white robes cutting the mistletoe from an oak with a golden sickle and catching it in a white cloak is well-known. In fact, mistletoe is rarely found growing on oaks, and it is probably this rare

A British Druid Standing by an Oak
(William Stukeley, 1740)

coupling of the plant, which grows midway between heaven and earth, with the thunder god's tree, that made it so special.

Long life is indicated by the dreaming of an oak tree, and the oak is traditionally associated with hospitality. It also stood as a symbol of renewal, which has led various people to use its energies therapeutically, such as the northern Native Americans. Apparently Bismark used to stand for half an hour leaning against an oak when feeling low for the same reason, and psychics or sensitives have even been known to hear an oak "singing". The special nature of the oak may also explain why it is host to more kinds of animals and plants than any other species of British tree. It is therefore a tree of much importance in the field of medicine, and perhaps Urswick used oak in the curing of Herne, and the foresters used oak branches when preparing his stretcher (see chapter *A Windsor Legend*). It was believed that when an oak was felled, it groaned or shrieked, and to cut one down was considered very unlucky, but to keep its branches or acorns in a house protected it from being struck by lightning. However, oak wood became even more powerful if the tree it had come from had itself been struck, and to stand under an oak gave one protection, not only from being struck but also from the power of witches.

Oak was used for fuel at the Celtic fire festivals of Lughnasa (August 1st), Samhain (November 1st), Imbolc (February 1st), and the most important Beltane (May 1st). The latter was held in honour of the solar god Bel or Belenos, whose name means "brightly shining", and the oak was sacred to him, being the midsummer tree flowering at the sun's peak of intensity. The god was also associated with the fertility of cattle, and there may well be a connection here with Herne in that Shakespeare tells us that he "takes the cattle and makes milch-kine yield blood." The web of interconnectedness in folklore and mythology may be telling us that these themes of oak/horned god/fertility/cattle are originally parts of an early myth.

Thor's Oak in Gaesmere, Germany, suffered a fatal attack in 723 CE at the hands of a manic English Christian named Boniface, who later gained sainthood. This missionary carried out a lot of conversion work in Germany, so much so that Pope Zacharias had to ask him to tone down his activities. The oak was an enormous specimen well revered by the local pagans who, however, impressed by his sacrilegious deed, became converts to the new Faith. St Boniface went on to become the Patron Saint of Germany.

Boniface Fells the Holy Oak (Carl Gottlieb Peschel, c.1860)

Moving further back in time to the Bronze Age, we find another example of the veneration of the oak in the form of a burial from Gristhorpe in Yorkshire. In 1834, beneath a large burial mound was discovered a large skeleton which had been place in an oak coffin, hewn out of the trunk and split in two to form a base and a top. Above the coffin, a quantity of oak branches had been placed together loosely. Perhaps it was hoped that the man's soul would live on with the aid of the magical oak. The Old Testament refers to the pagans' reverence of the oak, as this passage from Ezekiel (6.13) bears out:

"Then shall ye know that I am the Lord, when their slain men shall be among their idols round about their altars, upon every high hill, in all the tops of the mountains, and under every green tree, and under every thick oak, the place where they did offer sweet savour to all their idols."

In pre-Christian times, couples were sometimes married beneath Marriage Oaks, and remnants of this persisted into the Christian period when newlyweds would dance around such an oak, and cut a cross in its bark. A notable example of the association of the oak and the Faith is to be seen at the Chapel Oak in Allouville-Bellefosse in Normandy. Here grows a huge tree which contains within its hollow trunk an altar dedicated to the Virgin Mary, and it is still used twice a year for celebrating Mass.

To finish off this section – the sad story of the Whiteleaved Oak. This tree, or rather its remains, stands close to the hamlet of Whiteleaved Oak in the Malverns, Herefordshire, where this county has borders with Worcestershire and Gloucestershire. It was said that it bore white leaves, an early mention by a Henry Dingley in 1584 confirming this. However, an Edwin Lees in 1877 reported that it was not in existence any more, but it was remembered by the locals at that time, when its leaves were "variegated with white blotches."

Like the Glastonbury Thorn, it attracted visitors from far and wide, with gifts being left inside the oak, such as gems, jewels and the like. On its branches in the summer, people would dangle flowers, feathers, coloured ribbons and pentagrams, amongst other things. Its popularity even led to a visitor's book being introduced, which one could sign and add poems and other messages, but it eventually became too damaged and had to be removed. Nowadays, all this interest in locations with esoteric reputations often leads to the tarnishing and sometimes destruction of them. Now, however, the sad story of the tree's demise:

On July 5th, 2020, the Whiteleaved Oak, estimated to be around 500 years old, was burnt to ashes. The fire began about 11.30pm, and fire-fighters were called out, who battled through the night trying to save the tree, unfortunately in vain. The cause of the fire is not known, but it is a common practice by irresponsible and thoughtless people to place burning candles on such trees. Chief Druid King Arthur Pendragon's comment on the disaster was: "To see something like this happen to something that we revere, something that is so close to us spiritually, is very upsetting indeed." In fact, it was likely that the tree had died about three years prior to the fire, but its remains were still there for people to visit. A salutary tale.

HERNE'S OAK

First a note to point out that Windsor Great Park contains many oak trees, a few with names. The Conqueror's Oak is said to date back before the days of William the Conqueror, now just a trunk after being felled during the First World War. It was also a hanging tree for many centuries. Nearby is Offa's Oak, now with a split trunk, which still sprouts leaves even though some claim that it could be as old as 1,500 years, but not old enough to be living at the time of King Offa of Mercia who died in 796. In 1937, King George VI had 60 oak trees planted in the park, commemorating the King's coronation, the area being known as the King George VI Coronation Plantation. Twenty different species were planted by representatives of the 59 Commonwealth countries, all placed in places corresponding with the compass points of the varying parts of the British Empire lying in relation to the British Isles. But now we turn to Herne's Oak.

Venerable oaks were highly regarded in Saxon times, with some oaks living up to around 600 to 1,000 years, so even Herne's Oak could conceivably have been around in late Saxon times. The story of Herne's Oak and its situation is confused, with the original tree being felled, after which another tree was erroneously identified as the real tree, which then blew down in a storm, and ultimately the tree we see now was planted in 1906.

First the location of Herne's Oak in the Little Park, or Lydecroft Park, the element *lyde* deriving from the Anglo-Saxon word *hlyde* – a name for a stream meaning "loud", presumably the nearby stream being noisy. The second element is *croft* – denoting a "small enclosure". Now known as the Home Park, it is 655 acres in size, is run by the Crown Estate, and is private and not accessible to the public. The Frogmore Estate is also part of the Park, which includes The Royal Mausoleum where Queen Victoria and Prince Albert lie, and the Royal Burial Ground where Edward VIII, and latterly the Duke of Windsor, and Wallis Simpson, Duchess of Windsor, are buried (in 1972, this author remembers visiting the lying in state of Edward in St George's Chapel, joining a long queue). The boundaries of the park were fixed under the Windsor Improvement Act of 1846 and the Windsor Castle Act of 1848, when the previous road which once led through the park to the village of Datchet was closed off, and the public were thenceforth barred from what was once public land. Herne's Oak was situated north of Frogmore and east of the Long Walk.

In 1780, Richard Gough, a prominent antiquarian, was concerned that "there is no painting of Herne the Hunter's Oak and the Fairy Dell mentioned by Shakespeare, and still to be seen in Queen Elizabeth's walk in the Little Park." However, this was rectified over the following few years, with a number of sketches being made of the oak, by such artists as Paul Sandby and Samuel Ireland. All these reveal that the oak was a pollard, which involved the tree being lopped in the winter season when the ground was wet, in order that the deer were able to nibble the bark.

Herne's Oak was cut down in the spring of 1796, on the unwitting orders of George III who had commanded that all the trees in the Little Park be numbered. However, his bailiff pointed out that some of the trees were in fact dead, which led to the King's order to have them felled. The King's plan was to have some of the old trees in Windsor Great Park removed and replaced with new ones, Herne's Oak being inadvertently included in the felling programme. There were various opposing views on the reason for the felling. One claimed that the King instructed that it be felled due to one of his fits of madness, which he was renowned for.[1] An alternative view had it that he was fed up with people talking about the fact that indeed it was Herne's Oak.

George III of the United Kingdom
(Engraving by Henry Hoppner Meyer, 1817)
(National Portrait Gallery) (Public Domain, Wikimedia Commons)

However, he seems to have accepted that the tree had been cut down, as one story goes. Despite denying on several occasions that it had happened, he eventually admitted the error and said that he was very sorry for the oversight, as the ancient oak was highly regarded, not only by himself but also by the local townsfolk of Windsor. It had become a tourist attraction after the publication of *The Merry Wives of Windsor*, and after Queen Elizabeth I had

---

1   A pastime of his was taking watches and clocks apart and putting them back together again. One of his watches, made for him in 1808, thought to be one of fewer than 10 tourbillon watches known to exist, is valued at £2 million. He was probably bipolar, and eventually his eccentricities turned into dementia, and he died of pneumonia, blind and nearly deaf.

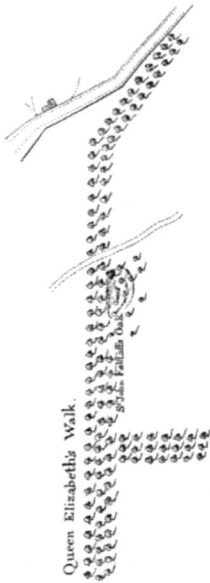

Part of a map of the Home Park in 1742, showing Sir John Falstaff's Oak

relaxed the laws relating to the royal parks. This enabled people to visit the Little Park more freely to view sites mentioned in the play. This freedom, however, was largely lost when James I ascended the throne and, wishing to hunt privately in the Great Park, had access to large areas made forbidden. Nevertheless, the locals regarded the park as common land, and no doubt many trespassers went unpunished. The oak was also called Falstaff's Oak, which can be found on the adjacent map.

The oak probably ended up stag-headed, which means that it had dead branches at its top sticking up above the green-leaved branches, looking rather like the antlers of a stag. It is said that oak trees, which sometimes show this feature, live a life of three stages: 300 years of growth, 300 years of rest, and finally 300 years of decline. The original Herne's Oak, when illustrated in the eighteenth century, was obviously in the latter stage and stag-headed, and if it had not been inadvertently cut down, it would not have lived that much longer.

The ancient oak itself was respected to such an extent that, after its felling, it was so sought after that the then president of the Royal Academy, Benjamin West, acquired a section of one of its knotty arms for himself. An ode to Herne's Oak was even composed (see below). There was also a local tradition that the spectral form of the tree was sometimes to be seen after its untimely demise, with Herne hanging from it – a ghostly tree haunting a fateful spot. Petry mentions a similar suicide by hanging from Aargau in Switzerland. This 1856 account also merges the hanging from an oak with the Wild Hunt:

> *"A keeper hanged himself on an oak in the beech wood on Kestenberg Hill between the castles of Wildegg and Brunnegg. When the lord of the castle found him there, moving backwards and forwards as the wind swayed the branches, he ordered that the tree should be felled: but as the axe cut into it, it oozed blood, there were red veins in the trunk. The people therefore burnt both the trunk and the corpse. Since that time, the dead man has stalked the wood as the wild huntsman of Wildegg. He hunts with spectral hounds, and one can often hear them yelping as he hangs them in the trees, straps and lashes them."*

As recorded above, this tale bears remarkable similarities to that of Herne, revealing what folklorists call motifs – which consist of repeated story-elements contained within diverse folktales from anywhere. Herne's Oak was situated close by the Fairies' Dell, a sunken feature with a reputed haunted path connecting the two. Dells are small valleys or hollows which are often cloaked by trees or turf, the word being related to "dale". The site of these in the Little Park is obviously a place steeped in local folklore, surfacing in *The Merry Wives of Windsor*, but over time the Dell became gradually filled in. However, Prince Albert, wishing to preserve the area's association with Shakespeare, decided to dig out the accumulated earth with a view to recreate the Fairies' Dell itself. As to the erroneously supposed Herne's Oak, which blew down in 1863, it was hoped that the memory of the tree could be maintained, thus leading to the carvings from its wood described below. A branch from this tree broke off in 1843, and was preserved in the royal stores at the castle.

Samuel Ireland (1744–1800) wrote the following in his 1792 work, *Picturesque Views on the River Thames*, dismissing the legend, stating that Herne was a real person, his suicide being seen as the origin of the haunting by his unquiet shade. His account of a seemly local figure could add credence to the theory:

> *"The story of this Herne, who was keeper in the forest in the time of Elizabeth, runs thus: 'That having committed some great offence, for which he feared to lose his situation and fall into disgrace, he was induced to hang himself on this tree. The credulity of the times easily worked on the minds of the ignorant to suppose that his ghost should haunt the spot.'"*

Herne's Oak (Samuel Ireland, 18c)

The search for the precise location of Herne's Oak has been outlined elsewhere (see Tighe & Davis), and a map of 1742 clearly marks the position of "Sir John Falstaff's Oak" adjacent to the edge of a pit. Interestingly this reference seems to indicate that the tree was known more for its appearance in Shakespeare's play than any tradition concerning Herne. No doubt the pit is that mentioned in the play, where Nan Page and her "fairies" are "all couched in a pit hard by Herne's Oak." After the restoration of the castle in the early nineteenth century, the rubble produced was dumped in the pit. This led local publisher, journalist and author, Charles Knight (1791–1873), to write the following:

"With our own recollection of the localities still vivid, we have recently visited the favourite haunts of our boyhood in the Little Park. Our sensations were not pleasurable. The spot is so changed, that we could scarcely recognize it. We lamented twenty-five years ago that the common footpath to Datchet should have been carried through the picturesque dell, near which all tradition agreed that Herne's Oak stood; but we were not prepared to find that, during the alterations to the castle, the most extensive and deepest part of the dell, all on the north of the path, has been filled up and made perfectively level. Our old favourite thorns are now all buried, and the antique roots of the old trees that stood in and about the dell are covered up. Surely the rubbish of the castle might have been conveyed to a less interesting place of deposit. The smaller shallower part of the dell, that on the south of the path, has been half filled up, and what remains is of a formal artificial character."

As far as I am aware, the pit, or dell, is no longer extant.

Sketches made of the original tree show it to have been a pollard, and these pictures, portrayed in its final years, depict it in an advanced stage of decay and to be quite hollow. A piece of local folklore claimed that no grass would grow around the tree – a theme to be found attached to other historic localities, such as Dragons' Hill near the Uffington White Horse. In 1783, the oak produced its last acorns; and in 1789, its last leaves. However, others were not of the opinion that this aged tree was Herne's Oak for, in 1838, another was cited as the real oak and, upon being blown down in 1863, Queen Victoria had it replaced. This was removed when the correct site was located in 1906.

Around the mid-nineteenth century, there was much debate about which tree was Herne's Oak, and here I add some interesting comments on the subject from the March 1841 *Gentleman's Magazine*, which begins with a contribution by someone who is just named as Plantagenet (actually a Dr Bromet). He starts by

HERNE THE HUNTER OF WINDSOR FOREST

stating that he had heard personally, and by letter, from "old, intelligent and respectable inhabitants of this town and vicinity," who assisted in his task of identifying the tree (which must have been the erroneous one blown down in 1863). He pointed out that he had painted it in 1822, which he contributed to the magazine in 1840, but it had changed its appearance so much since as an elm had fallen onto it. Continuing his account, he added that for those wishing to visit the tree in Windsor Little Park, this had been made easier as a Mr Jesse had installed a notice board to the tree with Shakespeare's verse:

> There is an old tale that Herne the hunter
> Some-time a keeper in Windsor forest,
> Doth all the winter time art full midnight
> Walk round about this Oak.

He then put forward the changing of the word 'this' to 'the', to distinguish it from the original tree. However, it appeared that the Little Park's bailiff and his labourers, two octogenarian widows, former hostesses of the White Hart and Garter, and the Castle inns, all were under the impression that the tree was Herne's Oak. Another woman recalled that, when she was a young girl, she used to dance around this tree believing it was the true oak, a charming reminiscence I think you will agree. This information was told to her by a keeper who had died 20 years previous at the age of 89, whose granddaughter had imparted this to her. And a recollection comes from a correspondent to the *Gentleman's Magazine* who said that as a singing-boy in 1786, he used he used to play in the park and often climbed into the tree's hollow trunk.

Having listened to all these points of view, he favoured George III's insistence that the real Herne's Oak was cut down in error in 1796. Plantagenet continued thus: "I must beg, in the absence of any document, most respectfully to doubt whether the King had better reasons for his statement than this 'tale delivered' to him, and 'received,' as in duty bound, by these about him, 'for a truth'."

In addition, he pointed out that the erroneous tree was chosen after the King's "lamented mental malady, and, possibly during some temporary excitement, which he caused; for, I am told, that the King was excessively annoyed by the obstinacy of the public, in not crediting his statement, and every opportunity to contradict their opinion [i.e. the bailiff and others] that an old oak, which had been felled by his, perhaps inadvertent, consent, was, really, the tree alluded to by Shakespeare." Furthermore, his "intelligent correspondent" distinctly recalled his father having received a seat and other items carved from its wood, and that the tree was the sole dead oak in the Little Park. Further evidence from Plantagenet was backed up by the following (apologies for the list format, this way is easier to follow):

a) A certain Charles Knight, a "no mean authority" on the subject, publically declared his opinion that the real Herne's Oak was felled some 50 or 60 years ago, though he could not tell exactly where the tree stood. This takes us back to roughly the time when the tree was cut down.

b) A bailiff at the castle mentioned that on an occasion when George III once entered the Queen's Lodge, he discovered that two chairs had been presented to him, which had been made from the wood of the deceased Herne's Oak. The King immediately threw them out, insisting that the tree was still in existence, which just shows how muddled his mind was becoming.

c) A "worthy" 84 year-old shopkeeper in Peascod Street in Windsor described that when he was a boy the hollow tree had been cut down about 45 years previously, which takes us back to 1796, the very year that it actually occurred. He also recalled standing close to the erroneous oak, and that both real oak and the erroneous one were still alive, with the latter being comparatively vigorous.

d) Another correspondent stated that when he was a boy the real tree was dead, and that it was so decayed that it was almost "a blotch" on the "surrounding verdure". Again, this would take us close to the end of the eighteenth century.

e) The father of the aforementioned singing-boy, a native of the nearby village of Datchet, was a Park Foreman who assisted in the chopping down and grubbing up of the tree. In addition, he stated that in 1783 his father collected an acorn from the tree which he hoped would have been planted "with due ceremony" on the site of the original tree.

f) Another native of Windsor asserted that as a boy a portion of Herne's Oak's root "big enough for a gun-stock" was given to him by the forester who actually cut the tree down.

g) A Miss Drewe of Datchet, now deceased, mentioned to a friend of Plantagenet that a few years prior the two of them had walked near the erroneous oak. Then there was no indication that the tree was called Herne's Oak until after the demolition of another old tree having that name which, she shrewdly pointed out, "would never probably become extinct for want of future claimants."

h) The two daughters of a physician, Dr Lind, a confident of King George, used to show visitors the remains of the old Herne's Oak and present it as that Shakespeare featured in his play.

i) A daughter of a Colonel Rooke, who lived at the castle for many years, said that her father was told by an old man that his grandfather used to speak often about Herne's Oak, the location of which he would point out at the edge of a gravel pit (the Fairies' Dell). This lady also recalled that her father's view was confirmed, as it must have been a very long time ago that the old man's grandfather imparted his knowledge to her father.

j) In 1788, a certain Rev. Howman became a resident of Windsor and made a drawing of the real oak. He then showed it to a celebrated artist named Francis Nicholson (1753–1844), who arranged for a lithographic print to be made of it in 1820. Whilst Howman was sketching the tree, Princess

Mary, and a lady with whom Howman was acquainted, appeared, and Princess Mary looked at his sketch. It was apparent to him that the Princess recognised that the tree he was sketching was indeed Herne's Oak.

k) Plantagenet then concluded the argument with what he felt was the final clincher. In a map of 1742, drawn by a resident who lived close to the castle and park, Sir John Falstaff's Oak is shown near the edge of the pit, concluding that it must have been also known locally as Herne's Oak (see map on page 54).

l) A Royal Huntsman, Charles Davis, recalled that in the early nineteenth century, when he was a young man, he used to perambulate around the fairy dell reading Shakespeare, whilst imagining himself amongst the fairies which appeared in the play.

Howman added that there were two people whom he highly regarded on this topic, namely the late Bishop of Salisbury, then Canon of Windsor, and the President of the Royal Academy, Mr West, then a Windsor resident. Both were of the opinion that they recognised the true oak when it was felled. Indeed, West was so concerned that "so great a curiosity should be removed" that he made a request to have a fragment of the wood as a relic. Furthermore, he listed a number of "eminent" personages who backed him up, including the then Dean of Windsor, Mr Cornewall, later Bishop of Worcester; Mr Majendie, later Bishop of Bangor; Mr Fisher, later Bishop of Salisbury; Dr Hallam, Dean of Bristol; and Mr Wilson, the Preceptor of Mr Pitt, amongst other respectable families whose ancestors had long resided in the Windsor area. For further support he referred to an article in the *Quarterly Review* concerning London's Arboretum et Fruticetum Britannicum, which was of the opinion that Howman's tree was the true original.

Howman's view was that "when a general opinion prevailed where men of eminence resided, it afforded a very strong presumption that it was founded on good authority, I am very certain that such a person ... would never have taken such an interest in the tree, unless he had been persuaded on the best authority that it really was that which Shakespeare has described." Also, Plantagenet was of the opinion that on the subject of the real Herne's Oak, "assertions of park-keepers and labourers should be cautiously received." So I shall leave it at that.

The Original Herne's Oak in 1783 (The Royal Windsor Forum)

So, we can now say that Herne's Oak was situated in the Little Park, and was also known as Sir John Falstaff's Oak, and was well favoured by the Windsor locals. Nevertheless, in 1838, a Deputy Surveyor-General of the Royal Parks, one Edward Jesse (1780-1868), argued that an oak which stood in the avenue of trees in the Little Park was the true Herne's Oak. He was an author on natural history, including *A Summer's Day at Windsor*, and *A Visit to Eton* (1841), and he was well known for his opinion on the oak, which attracted many supporters, including Queen Victoria herself.

The full story of the 1863 demise of the wrong oak is as follows. A newspaper report from Saturday, 5th September, 1863, described how "the shattered trunk of Herne's Oak" was blown

Queen Victoria, 15th May, 1860
(J.J.E. Mayall, Wikimedia Commons)

down on Monday morning. Consequently, it was important to report this to Queen Victoria, who at the time was in Germany. She immediately ordered that the trunk should not be removed until she returned to the castle. Whilst she travelled back to England, a day and night watch over the trunk was arranged to deter souvenir hunters. On the morning after her return, she, along with lesser members of the royal family, visited the site, and the queen was adamant that the tree be treated as Herne's Oak. The accepted view of Herne at this time was that he had been a forest keeper in the early part of Queen Elizabeth's reign, when he committed some offence. Angered by this, Elizabeth dismissed him immediately and he "formed the desperate resolution to hang himself upon this tree."

The erroneous Herne's Oak just before its demise in 1863

The erroneous Herne's Oak, which blew down in a storm in 1863, was cut up and from it many objects carved into souvenirs, one special item being a compartmented casket made in an Elizabethan style. This was carved by a William Perry, Wood Carver to the Queen, who wrote: "A treatise on the identity of Herne's Oak, showing the maiden tree to have been the real one," and described the casket as a receptacle to house "relics, or interesting memoranda relating to the immortal Bard." These included the first collected edition of Shakespeare's Poems published in 1640, and the still more rare of his Dramatic Works published in 1623. On the inside of the drop front is a silver plaque containing an inscription detailing the casket's provenance and the name of William Perry, carver, and the date 1866, the plaque stating:

> *"The old tree fell down in 1863, a portion being most graciously given by HER MAJESTY QUEEN VICTORIA to MISS BURDETT*

COUTTS, for the purpose of encasing volumes which are – 'Not for an age, but for all time.'"[2]

At the corners are niches, each displaying an oak tree in bas relief in the background, together with ivy creeping around the trunks. The niches contain in full relief figures from *The Merry Wives of Windsor*, Falstaff, Ann Page and two other minor characters. The centre of the top features a portrait of the Bard with the inscription "Shakespeare", together with his dates. The front of the casket contains the Arms of Miss Burdett Coutts, and the monogram A.G.B.C. (Angela Georgina Burdett-Coutts), while the back has the shield and crest of Shakespeare. The ends show the monograms W.S. and A.H. – i.e. William Shakespeare and Ann Hathaway. In addition, stars, torches and jewels are depicted in the decoration, signifying the brightness, glory and value of the works contained inside. Queen Victoria also had a cabinet made from the timber; and, as you will expect, Herne's Oak carvings are highly collectable.

William Perry's Casket (Fine Art America)

---

2   Angela Georgina Burdett-Coutts (1814–1906) was an outspoken philanthropist. Edward VII said of her, "After my mother, she is the most remarkable woman in the Kingdom."

In Perry's Treatise he spends 63 detailed pages in trying to persuade readers that the tree which blew down in 1863 was the true Herne's Oak. His evidence included the suggestion that George IV was also of the opinion that the Herne's Oak cut down in 1796 was not the true oak at all. Perry stated that at the end of the Treatise:

> "Surely, courteous reader, taking every fact in connexion with this 'time-destroyed', 'withered' tree, into consideration, there remains scarcely a loophole through which you may escape believing; and you will cordially unite with me in the opinion I entertain, that the venerable tree which on the last day of August, 1863, fell to the ground from natural decay, was, undoubtedly, the oak around which the Hunter walked – was, in truth, HERNE'S OAK."

The Search for Herne the Hunter, by George Cruikshank
The steel-engraving depicts Henry VIII's workers trying to raze Herne's Oak, where Herne sought refuge. The King was determined to eradicate Herne the Hunter.
(Philip V. Allingham, Victorian Web)
The engraving shows Captain Bouchier in uniform with a spear, behind whom Henry VIII is seen, mounted on a horse.

I surmise that, as Perry carved items from this tree, it irked him that others considered that it was not the true oak, so he tried to convince himself that he had indeed worked on the correct tree's wood.

The purpose of destroying Herne's Oak in Ainsworth's novel was to eradicate Herne's safe haven, which leads to the perception that Herne is flesh and bone, rather than a spectral spirit. The queen apparently stuck to the theory that this was indeed Herne's Oak and had the Royal Upholsterer, a certain Mr Goetz, make mementos such as chairs, cabinets and worktables from the tree. There is still in existence a three volume set of the complete works of Shakespeare bound in wood from the oak. A receipt for this reads: "Binding wood from Herne's Oak, £3 3s" and the cover is engraved with "Herne's Oak blown down in the Home Park, August 31, 1863." It was said that after its demise, logs were gathered up and were burned at the castle "to burn away the ghost of Herne the Hunter." In addition, one log was saved and a woodcarver got to work on it, creating a bust of Shakespeare himself. This can be viewed at the Guildhall Museum in Windsor High Street (see below).

This author has an old *Windsor Express* newspaper cutting with no date, but it looks like sometime in the 1960s, which adds further information on the erroneous tree and its demise. It concerns an oil painting of the tree which was painted by R.A. Collins (died in 1847) and was owned by one Dennis Lightfoot of Chestnuts, Hatch Lane in Windsor. Also possessed by Mr Lightfoot was the three volume set of the complete works of Shakespeare mentioned above, edited by Howard Staunton, and artistically bound in wood from the tree. Both the painter and the books belonged to Maurice Lightfoot, father of Dennis, a previous editor of the *Express*, who bought the books at an auction. The previous owner was George Tuck of Victoria Street. The article, from the *Express* dated Saturday, September 5th, 1863, added how "the

shattered trunk of Herne's Oak" was blown down on Monday morning.

The late Michael Bayley, a Maidenhead historian, had in his possession a chunk of the original Herne's Oak, which was passed on to him by the great great great granddaughter of the man who felled the tree. It was one of three chips which a Mr Tarrant (a member of an old Eton family) and two other foresters were allowed to keep (see below).

The caption on the base of the stand on which the piece of wood is held is as follows:

A piece of the Oak of Herne the Hunter cut down between 1792 & 1800 by Mr Tarrant & 2 other men on orders from King George III each man being allowed to keep two pieces of wood.

A further item made from the wood of the false oak can be seen in Egham Museum, in the form of a paperknife, with the handle made from the tree. It has an inscription which reads:

MADE FROM HERNE'S OAK WINDSOR FOREST
BLOWN DOWN ON AUGUST 31st 1864

Of course, the tree blew down on 31st August 1863, which makes one wonder if the wood came from either of the two Herne's Oaks. In the *Illustrated News* on 24th September, 1863, it was reported that people were so desperate to own wood from the tree that it was guarded 24/7.

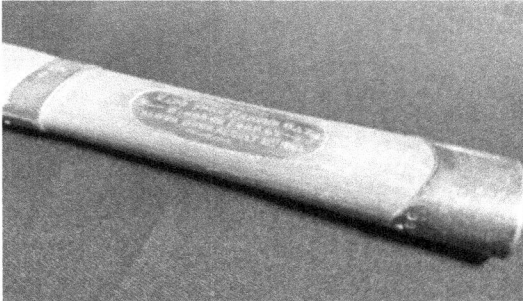

Photo from Egham Museum

The tip of the knife is engraved with a 7-pointed crown and "*ES 1887*" – the two initials being thought to refer to Baroness Schroeder, but any further information as to how she acquired the knife is not known. It was donated to Egham Museum by Helene Dorothee Eveline Emma Schroeder, the great-niece of the Baroness, who resided in the Egham environs all her life, and she was involved with the Egham-by-Runnymede Historical Society.[3]

---

3 Nearby is Runnymede, where Magna Carta was signed by King John in 1215.

The Schroeder family were a well-off family who came from Hamburg, now in Germany, and were allowed to use the terms "Baron" and "Baroness" whilst living in Britain, and they lived in Manor House, Dell Park, Englefield Green from 1825. It is unknown how the knife came to be possessed by the Schroeder family, but Helene eventually donated it to Egham Museum.[44]

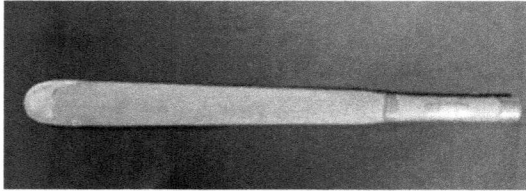

Photo from Egham Museum

Returning to the confusion about the two trees – in the ensuing years, much research was carried out and eventually King Edward VII had the matter looked into thoroughly, the original site being settled once and for all. The remains of the tree which fell down in 1863 were dug up and the Little Park's avenue was replanted. On 29th January, 1906, Herne's Oak 2 was planted exactly on the site of the original oak. It is of interest to note that Edward VII, who died in 1910, was buried dressed in full military uniform in a huge oak coffin in St George's Chapel.

King Edward VII, 1902
(Public Domain)

---

4   Information on and photos of the paper knife, by kind permission from Egham Museum.

Herne's Oak 2 (Crown Estate)

Thus the history of the "Herne's Oaks" and their timelines can be summarised as follows:

1796   The inadvertent felling of the original Herne's Oak by George III.

1838   Edward Jesse concluded that an oak tree growing just south of the original was Herne's Oak.

1863   This erroneously named tree, accepted as the true one by Queen Victoria, blew down on 31st August.

1863   Queen Victoria planted a replacement on the site of the erroneous tree on 12th September.

1906   The replacement was cut down when the Home Park Avenue was replanted.

1906   Edward VII planted another oak on the site of the original tree on 29th January (Herne's Oak 2).

The commemorative plaque on Herne's Oak 2 reads as follows:

THIS TREE WAS PLANTED 29TH. JANUARY 1906 BY COMMAND OF HIS MAJESTY THE KING EDWARD VII TO MARK THE ORIGINAL POSITION OF "HERNE'S OAK".

IN 1796 THIS OAK, BEING DEAD, WAS CUT DOWN WITH OTHER DEAD TREES IN THE PARK AND ITS NAME WAS TRANSFERRED TO ANOTHER OLD OAK STANDING A FEW PACES TO THE SOUTH.

THE SECOND "HERNE'S OAK" WAS BLOWN DOWN 31ST. AUGUST 1863 AND IN ITS PLACE A NEW TREE WAS PLANTED BY HER MAJESTY QUEEN VICTORIA 12TH. SEPTEMBER 1863.

IN REPLANTING THE AVENUE IN 1906 THE NEW TREE HAD TO BE REMOVED.
ITS COMMORATIVE INSCRIPTION HAS BEEN RESET ON THE BACK OF THIS STONE.

The earlier inscription stated:

THIS TREE WAS PLANTED BY
HER MAJESTY QUEEN VICTORIA,
SEPTEMBER 12, 1863,
TO MARK THE SPOT WHERE HERNE'S OAK STOOD.
THE OLD TREE WAS BLOWN DOWN
AUGUST 31, 1863.

THERE IS AN OLD TALE GOES THAT HERNE THE HUNTER,
SOMETIME KEEPER HERE AT WINDSOR FOREST,
DOTH ALL THE WINTER TIME AT STILL MIDNIGHT,
WALK ROUND ABOUT THE OAK.
– SHAKESPEARE

The verse comprises the first four lines from Mistress Page's account of Herne in *The Merry Wives of Windsor*. The reference to the "Old Tree" having been blown down seems to indicate that the plaque was placed at the site of the erroneous tree, but the first line mentions "this tree" as though it were still standing, which is puzzling.

All the illustrations of Herne's Oak between 1780 and 1796 reveal it to have been a pollard – a practice that took place in the winter when there was snow on the ground, in order that the royal deer were able to feed on the bark. I am grateful to the Crown Estate (in 2018) for confirming that Herne's Oak 2 is still standing, for providing the photo above, and being pleased to report that it is also thriving. However, it is situated in the private section of the Home Park, which is not accessible to the public.

Such was the affection the locals had for Herne's Oak, that even after its demise it was said that the shadowy form of the ill-fated tree was sometimes seen where it once stood, and the ghostly image of Herne's body was also witnessed swinging from its spectral branches. The late 2nd Earl of Gowrie, and former Conservative Party politician, also added his opinion on Herne's origins. He spent a number of his childhood years at the castle and viewed Herne as a folkloric legend featuring the survival of a fertility god; and Angus MacNaghten, author of *Haunted Berkshire*, goes along with this interpretation, surmising the existence of forest shrines, looked over by ancient priests. He considers that their rituals involved the wearing of headdresses adorned with antlers, and that Herne is a folk memory from pagan times, discussed in the chapter *Pagan Portals*.

In 1876, a firm known as the Old Windsor Tapestry Manufactory was established, which was housed in a now demolished building named Manor Lodge in Old Windsor. It was founded by two Frenchmen, Henri C.J. Henry (Director) and Marcel Brignolas (Manager), the business being a part of the Arts & Crafts movement of the late nineteenth century. The only other such establishment turning out tapestries contemporaneously, though, was that of William Morris, which was founded at Merton Abbey in 1881.

An early commission to depict scenes from *The Merry Wives of Windsor*, including the legend of Herne, was designed by the artist T.W. Hay. After completion, the scenes were displayed at the Paris Exhibition in 1878, followed by an exhibition at Windsor Guildhall in December of that year. Eight scenes were depicted, one featuring Herne's Oak, alluding to Act V, Scene V, in which Falstaff appears in the Fairy Dell hard by the Oak. The scene shows him surrounded by Anne Page as Queen of the Fairies, her troop of masked fairies, and eleven other figures, making up quite a complex scenario. Falstaff himself is shown wearing stag's antlers on his head, crouching down with his face lit up by the fairies' torches. In the background, Herne's Oak is shown, with Windsor Castle on the skyline. A summer night's revel is portrayed, lit by the fairies' torches, with the green leaves as a backdrop to Anne Page, framing her bower. The whole tapestry is eight feet eight inches by six feet, and the tapestries won a gold medal at The Paris Exhibition of 1878.

The year before the tree's demise, an historic event occurred. German royalty, along with other German notables, including Frederick William V of Prussia and the polymath Baron Humboldt, attended the baptism of the Prince of Wales in November 1841 – the future King Edward VII. Whilst staying in Windsor, they expressed a desire to see Herne's Oak. Gathered at the tree, obviously the erroneous one, they all stood for a while in silence, and before departing, they were allowed to pluck ivy leaves from the tree's trunk as mementoes. Such was the fame of the tree through the Shakespeare connection. Herne's Park attracted "pilgrims" from all over the world.[5] However, the tree must have been well-known before *The Merry Wives of Windsor*

---

5 Simon Young in *Herne, the Windsor Bogey, Gramarye journal*, issue 12, Winter 2017.

was first performed, since a map published by John Norden, drawn up about 1597, shows a copse labelled as Herne's Wood, five years before the play was registered for publication in 1602.

It is always pleasing to see children appreciating local history and folklore; and in 2017, Windsor & Maidenhead Borough Museum held an exhibition titled Tree Tales from the Great Park, which included an event for children to mould a model of a tree and to explore the legend of Herne the Hunter and Herne's Oak. A copy of my book *In Search of Herne the Hunter* was on display, adding to the interest for the locals of Windsor and those from afar.

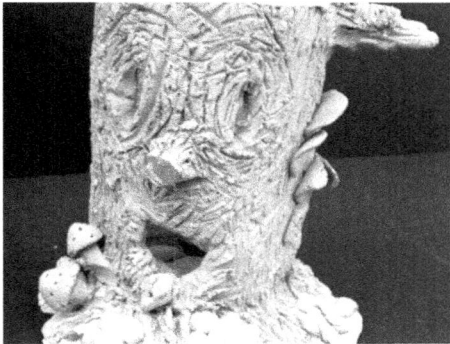

A model tree made by one of the children
(*Maidenhead Advertiser*)

And to end this section, an ode to the demise of the tree was published in the *Whitehall Evening Post*, a London newspaper founded in 1718 by Daniel Defoe, of *Robinson Crusoe* fame:

Upon Herne's Oak Being Cut Down in the Spring of 1796

"Within this dell, for many an age,
Herne's Oak uprear'd its antique head -
Oh! most unhallow'd was the rage
Which tore it from its native bed!

The storm that stript the forest bare
Would yet refrain this tree to wrong,
And Time himself appear'd to spare
A fragment he had known so long.

'Twas marked with popular regard,
When fam'd Elizabeth was queen;
And Shakespeare, England's matchless bard,
Made it the subject of a scene.

So honour'd when in veruredrest,
To me the wither'd trunk was dear;
As, when the warrior is at rest,
His trophied armour men revere.

That nightly Herne walk'd round this oak,
The superstitious eld receiv'd;
And what they of his outrage spoke,
The rising age in fear believ'd.

The hunter in his morning range,
Would not the tree with lightness view;
To him, Herne's legend, passing strange,
In spite of scoffers, still seem'd true.

Oh, where were all the fairy crew
Who revels kept in days remote,
That round the oak no spell they drew,
Before the axe its fibres smote?

Could wishes but ensure the power,
The tree again its head should rear
Shrubs fence it with a fadeless bower,
And these inscriptive lines appear, -

'Here, as wild Avon's poet stray'd -
Hold! let me check this feeble strain -
The spot by Shakespeare sacred made,
A verse like mine would not profane.'"

HERNE'S OAK PUBLIC HOUSE

Inn sign of the Herne's Oak public house

For many a year there was a public house named Herne's Oak in the nearby village of Winkfield (Wineca's field), but unfortunately it is no longer an inn, as the building has been converted into offices; however, the building has an interesting history. The structure appears to have been built in the late sixteenth century or sometime in the seventeenth century, the earliest extant deed dating from 1752, which refers to a messuage (a dwelling with out-houses), a barn, garden, orchard, as well as six acres of pasture, six acres of meadows and one acre of woodland.

In 1764, the property changed hands for a sum of £60, when it was described as edifices, buildings, bar, stables, outhouses, orchard, garden and easements together with curtilages (areas of land attached to a house) and two closes or crofts of arable land pasture/meadow containing three acres. But the deeds make no mention of brewing, a beer-house or the name The Herne's Oak. After several changes of hands, the property was acquired in 1820 by a John Tull, a Windsor baker, still without mention of the name. In 1826, a John Jennings bought the property and it is assumed, as his occupation was that of a brewer, that it was he who turned it into a public house and named it The Herne's Oak.

The Jennings family auctioned the property in 1862, with three acres of land and four houses, at The Star & Garter in Windsor, which went under the hammer to the brewer, Lawrence Wethered, when the property was first officially referred to as The Herne's Oak. Later, Strong's Brewery took over, followed by Whitbread, which owned the premises until it was sold off in 2009. "Harry" Harrison, the landlord in the latter years, used to have a brief summary of Herne the Hunter's story pinned up inside the pub (see below). There is also a local Winkfield legend that the ghost of Herne has been encountered outside the premises, but other than that, I have not been able to discover why the name was chosen, as it was some three miles from the tree itself.

The inn after closing down (Valerie Fitch)

Just before its demise, my wife Valerie managed to take a photograph of the last inn-sign, which was quite different from the one that I photographed for my first Herne book, and I reproduce it here (it is not known why the figure of Herne has not been portrayed with his antlers though).

It is sad that an old pub with its Windsor Forest and Herne associations has had to go, but I suppose it is a sign of the times. At the auction of 1862, the title to the house was the same as that of The Herne's Oak, when the estate was split into lots. It could well be, therefore, that the legends surrounding Herne's House may well relate to the pub. It must be pointed out that Herne's House is in private ownership and thus the owners' privacy must be observed.

The last inn sign – but why no antlers?
(Valerie Fitch)

Adjacent to the Winkfield pub, there was also a Herne's Cottage, now Herne's House, reputed to have been a Royal Park keeper's cottage in Henry VIII's time, with local legend stating that it was inhabited by Herne himself. It is conjectured that Nell Gwynn may have once owned it, as it was rumoured that she owned a nearby farm where she lived for a time; she certainly had other property, such as 61–63 King's Cross Road in London, which later became the popular Bagnigge Wells Spa. From 1680 to her death in 1687, she was given by Charles II the freehold of Burford House near the Home Park, 250 yards from the castle – so it is possible that Herne's Cottage was once her property. Nell Gwynn's house can be found in Church Street near the castle, now a Chinese restaurant (see photo below).

5 and 6 Church Street, Windsor (Nell Gwynn's House)
(Paul the Archivist, Wikimedia Commons)

I have also discovered that there was once a pub named The Herne's Oak in Windsor itself, which was situated in Rectory Terrace, Parsonage Lane. The 1871 census shows a Mary A. McCarthy in residence, who was referred to as a beer-seller, with her family. In 1901, the census recorded a William G. King occupying the premises, along with his family, and, in this case, he was called a beer retailer. In 1891, the occupants were described as gardeners, but after 1901 it doubled as a general store and has now been converted into a local shop, but I have not been able to find any more of its history.[6]

And to end this section, I should like to quote a notice that was displayed in the Herne's Oak inn, as told by the landlord "Harry" Harrison in 1999[7]:

> *"The ghost of Herne the Hunter roams the trees of the ancient forest of Windsor. Once a royal huntsman he became a favourite of the King when he saved the life of the monarch from a charging stag. Fatally wounded in his act of bravery Herne lay dying from his wounds when an old wizard appeared from within the trees. Pointing to Herne he spoke, 'if that life you wish to save then those there antlers to his head you must tie.' The King gave the order for the dead stag's antlers to be cut and placed on the head of Herne. As the life returned to this once limp body the old wizard disappeared. The favours shown by the King made the huntsmen envious and tales of untruth and hatred left their tongues. Herne was soon dismissed from service. Sad and dishonoured he went out into the forest and took his own life. Hanging from an old oak tree was found the lifeless body. From that day this tree was to be known as the HERNE'S OAK."*

Thus this concludes the story of a traditional English pub with its own legendary history, gone the way of so many others.

Works Consulted

The Winkfield Chronicles. Winkfield History Project Group Publishers (2000).

---

6 © 2021 pubwiki.co.uk (Directory of Pubs in the UK).
7 *The Winkfield Chronicles*, p101.

Herne the Hunter: A Berkshire Legend, by Michael John Petry (1972).
Annals of Windsor, Volumes 1 and 2, by R. Tighe and J. Davis (1858).
A Treatise on the Identity of Herne's Oak, Showing the Maiden Tree to Have Been the Real One, by William Perry (1867).

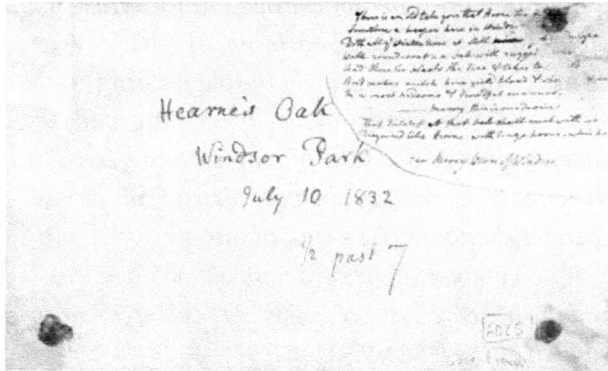

Reverse of a painting (above) sold by Abbott and Holder in May, 2022 (ref: 10466a), when it was described as: "Berkshire; 'Hearne's Oak, Windsor Park' [*sic*].

Pencil and watercolour. Inscribed verso and dated, 'July 10 1832 / 1/2 past 7'. Further inscribed with the lines from Shakespeare's *The Merry Wives of Windsor*. 5.25×8.5 inches." (Creator: William Crotch, Wikimedia Commons)

Stags and Antlers

HISTORY

Shakespeare described Herne's antlered headdress as "great ragg'd horns", but what was the significance of the antlers? The horns of bulls have been revered in many cultures, such as on Minoan Crete (*c.*2700–1100 BCE), and were symbolic of their owner's strength and power, as seen in the figure of the Minotaur. The Cretans saw the bull as a symbol of masculine fertility, and believed that the horns contained his vitality, probably due to their rapid growth. Their rites involved offering a bull's head complete with horns to the sky god. Horns were also associated with the moon, due to their similarity with the lunar crescent, and thus became linked to worship of lunar goddesses, such as the Roman Luna, who drove a chariot pulled by two horned oxen.

Antlers, however, were a special case, as their yearly renewal and idiosyncratic shape were linked with the theme of rebirth common to a number of religions. For instance, in the Christian faith, the date of Easter, a time of rebirth as in the Resurrection, is celebrated on the first Sunday after the first full moon on or after the spring equinox. To help understand the full significance of animals such as deer to early humans, and the special regard they had for their antlers, it will be necessary to delve into the realms of prehistoric archaeology and folklore.

We begin with an ancient burial dating back to the dawn of modern humanity. In a cave called Jebel Qafzeh near Nazareth in Israel, excavations revealed fossil human remains of individuals who are anatomically the same as ourselves, but who lived about 100,000 years ago. Most remarkable was that two skeletons, one of which was a boy aged about 12 or 13, had been buried clutching a set of fallow deer antlers. Such finds seem to indicate a deliberate interment involving a belief in an afterlife of some sort, the antlers no doubt symbolising rebirth and a new life. It is one of the earliest examples we have of ritual behaviour, and it is highly appropriate to this study that antlers were used in religious practices at such an early date.

Five stags with varied length of antlers resting in a forest
(Wellcome Collection Gallery, Wikimedia Commons)

Moving forward to Palaeolithic Europe during the Ice Age, we visit the wonderful pictures painted inside the caves of Lascaux in France and Altimira in Spain. It is apparent from such cave art that the red deer was a major food source for these people, as there are many depictions of this species amongst all the other animals which appear on the walls. Some picture them being hunted with bows and arrows, whilst others show them running and even swimming. Reindeer were also of prime importance, and there are indications that there may have been domesticated herds, which would have provided an abundant food supply. Interpretations of the artwork included that of hunting magic, and later that they were made by shamans. These would access the dark caves, some of which went a very long way, and would enter into a trance, perhaps with the aid of drugs. When they were ready, they would paint images of what they had "seen" in their visionary state.

The earliest antlers found in Britain to have been fashioned by humans are particularly relevant to the legend of Herne the Hunter. About 11,000 years ago in the Mesolithic era, or middle

Stone Age, a small band of hunter-gatherers settled one winter at Star Carr in the Vale of Pickering, Yorkshire. Here they set up a lakeside camp on a muddy slope where they constructed a platform of branches and brushwood which was used as a landing stage for their canoes. The importance of hunting to this community was apparent from the animal remains excavated from the site; the bones of many species being present, including aurochs, wolves, boars, foxes and beavers, as well as birds such as cranes and storks. More interesting was the large volume of deer remains, such as roe deer, elk and red deer; the latter especially so with 102 antlers surviving, of which 83 had been cut to produce splinters used to make barbed points for spears and harpoons.

However, the relevance of Star Carr to this study is the survival of 24 stag skulls with parts of the antlers still attached. They had all been worked in such a way as to make them lighter. Much of the beam had been cut away, and what was left had been hollowed out. The inside of the cranium had also been gouged out to make the skull thinner, and there was obviously an intention to remove as much as of the weighty bone as possible. But what made these stag frontlets so intriguing were the two perforated holes made in each of the temples, which could only have been used for one purpose – to pass thongs through to enable them to be tied somewhere, presumably someone's head. So here we can envisage antlered figures looking out at us from the distant past – primeval forerunners of Herne himself.

But as to the reason for donning these headdresses, there are three schools of thought. One is merely practical and suggests that the antlers were worn whilst hunting deer, perhaps being used as decoys, but this view is not likely, and the finding of so many together in one deposit hints at other uses. The second view is of a ritual function, the suggestion being that they were worn, perhaps along with deerskins, during dances which were aimed at ensuring the abundance of the deer herds and/or the fertility of nature in general. The author leans towards this theory.

Reconstruction of antler head-dress from Star Carr (British Museum)

The third view is the one held by more archaeologists today, which connects their usage with shamanism. The figure of the shaman was highly regarded in prehistoric and later communities, and they were considered to act as "medicine men", to use an outdated term, as well as being able to converse with the "spirit world" and impart their findings to the community via entering a trance state. The spirits would often be those of animals, which sometimes led to the shaman feeling himself actually becoming an animal. Such shamanic practices are normally associated with indigenous and tribal folk, gaining the power of healing the sick, and to accompany the souls of the deceased into the afterlife – rather like a psychopomp, similar to the Greek god Hermes. The only problem with this idea is the question: why were there as many as 24 headdresses found, unless the community was a shamanic school?

Portrayal of a Siberian shaman (17c) (Wikimedia Commons)

Turning to Germany, an excavation at Stellmoor near Hamburg produced a most interesting discovery. It appears that a group of reindeer hunters camped at the edge of a lake, much in the same manner as their contemporaries at Star Carr. Although no stag frontlets were discovered there, what was unearthed became of special importance. Close to the shore, a pinewood pole nearly seven feet long was found which was pointed at one end and blunt at the other, upon which was mounted a reindeer skull complete with antlers. Nearby were twelve more skulls with antlers, no doubt previous occupants of the end of the pole, and it seems that the ritual pole was stuck in the ground at the water's edge with the antlers on display. But what purpose did this prehistoric totem pole serve? We find the answer with the accompanying deposits discovered nearby.

Twelve whole reindeer had been submerged in the lake, all weighed down by having large stones placed in their abdomens. In addition, the skulls of 30 others were found in association with large stones, signifying further ritual deposits. They appear to belong to young does, some possibly pregnant, which were offered to the lake deities; and in addition, the remains of 650 other reindeer were discovered. Also, a straight line of complete reindeer skeletons was found, all with arrowheads embedded in their upper abdomens. Perhaps we can envisage a shaman slitting open the abdominal cavity with his flint knife, placing the stone within, and then sewing it up again with sinew. Then, amongst ceremonies which must remain a mystery to us, the animal was deposited in the lake. The Mesolithic culture that performed these rituals is known as the Ahrensburger, named after the nearby town of Ahrensburg.

The development of the antlers tells us that this occurred around May/June, and perhaps these people inaugurated the commencement of the season's hunting with the sacrifice of their first fruits. The fact that the victims were all female may have indicated hunting magic to ensure the plentiful supply of reindeer or, alternatively, the watery grave may have had some special significance for water, which has always been associated with fertility. But it may have been that their god was thought to reside underground and the ritual deposited was an attempt to make the offerings reach the deity. Whatever the precise reason, there is no doubt as to the preoccupation with deer and their antlers, a phenomenon which did not stop with these Mesolithic hunters.

Moving on to the Neolithic Age, red deer antlers were used as picks when constructing their monuments, but these were discarded after use. However, others were buried deliberately in structures, an example being the Lesser Cursus near Stonehenge where at the west end of the monument several antlers were discovered. This was no random deposit, for each antler had been purposely buried in the structure's ditch at regular intervals before the ditch was backfilled. All that can be said about cursi is that they might be of a ritual nature, and the meaning of the antlers deposit lost to us.

The answer to this question is probably connected to the growing and shedding of antlers and their rapid growth, increasing in size each year, which would have been seen as a source of wonder for ancient humans. In Britain, the indigenous species are red deer and roe deer. The latter's antlers are small compared with those of the red deer, whose antlers can grow up to twelve points, when the animal is known as a royal stag (male deer alone bear antlers, except in the case of reindeer and the caribou of North America). The rapid yearly growth with the use of the antlers during the mating season must have led to their veneration as sexual and fertility symbols from early times and be the reason why they are found in ancient burials.

At Chaldon Herring in Dorset, a barrow excavated in the mid nineteenth century revealed a deeply cut grave containing the inhumations of both an adult male and female, who had been buried in either a crouched or sitting position with stag antlers resting on their shoulders. Another similarly positioned skeleton, also with antlers, was found in an adjoining barrow. An excavation of a burial site at Amesbury near Stonehenge produced fifteen antlers placed at the foot and head of the skeleton; and at Hunter's Barrow (also in Wiltshire) a cremation was accompanied by the skeleton of a dog, and five finely made arrowheads surrounded by a wreath of antlers. Again, in that prehistoric area of Wiltshire, a pit excavated at Winklebury Camp revealed not only a complete red deer skeleton, but also those of twelve foxes. And at Stonehenge itself, over 100 antlers have been recovered from the ditch which surrounds the site. Further afield, in a tomb excavated on the tiny island of Holm of Papa Westray North in the Orkneys, were more than a dozen pairs of antlers. The magical power of antlers appears to have been seen by the Neolithic peoples as being of some benefit to the dead, as all these examples indicate.

Now we visit Grimes Graves, the Neolithic flint mines in Norfolk. Covering over 34 acres, the mines consist of 360 shafts, a few of which are open to the public, and this author can recommend a visit. Red deer antlers were the main tool used in digging the mines, but one shaft was found to hold perhaps England's most significant ritual deposit. A shaft had been quarried but had proved to be unproductive. To ensure that future shafts should be more successful, an altar had been set up by the miners in front of a ledge, upon which was placed a carved chalk figurine in the likeness of an obviously pregnant woman. Antlers were heaped around and on top of the flint pile, and next to this array were also found several flint balls and a chalk phallus. It seems unlikely that the antlers in this configuration were merely examples of the miners' tools, and they appear to have had some religious significance. The phallus and figurine have obvious fertile aspects, combining to influence the underground chambers to yield more flint.[1]

Similarly, at the Neolithic henge of Maumbury Rings in the Dorset town of Dorchester, another find was unearthed, consisting of ritual deposits. Here a number of flint balls and large, chalk phalli were discovered in close association with two antlered skulls. In 2016, a red deer skull and antlers were found on a beach at Borth in Wales, dating back 4,000 years – a rare find in that country. The antlers were four feet wide, and they belonged to a huge stag, which once roamed the land in the Bronze Age. In addition, stumps of yew and oak trees were uncovered on the same beach, leading to the fact that there was once a forest in the region – thus connecting again to the theme of sacred trees, Windsor Forest and Herne's Oak.

Mythologist and Classical scholar, Robert Graves, felt that the set of antlers found at the Neolithic tomb of Newgrange in Ireland were part of the sacred king's headdress, and that the stag was the royal beast of the Danaans tribe, the stag being well represented in Irish mythology.[2] The burial of antlers was

---

1 It has been suggested that this display was faked by young archaeologists at the 1939 excavations to trick the dig director, Leslie Armstrong, but nothing has ever come of this.

2 *The White Goddess*, by Robert Graves (1952). The Danaans were the people of the goddess Danu, a supernatural race who could also interact with mortals. Modern scholars treat Graves' interpretations of myth and prehistory as suspect, but this author believes that in dismissing all Graves' writings on such subjects, they are throwing out the baby with the bath water.

not confined to prehistoric times, however, and an interesting survival from Roman Britain is worth mentioning. Two sets were discovered at the base of a pit excavated at Wasperton in Warwickshire. They had been carefully positioned in the form of a square, the centre of which produced evidence that a fire had been lit. Under this arrangement was carved the Latin word FELICITER, meaning "for luck". This use of antlers, even though a continuation of an ancient tradition, seems here to have deteriorated into just a good luck charm. At the Romano-British temple at Brean Down in Somerset, a smaller building adjacent to the main temple contained a store of antlers, their presence indicating ritual usage continuing over the millennia.

The deer features to a large extent in British mythology, especially in the form of the White Hart or Hind, which was sacred to the Druids of Britain. Both Pwll, Lord of Dyfed, and Sir Galahad of the Arthurian legends are said to have had encounters with white stags, whose appearances usually led mythical heroes into otherworldly realms. Mythologically, the White Hart symbolises the luring of the horned god into her sacred grove. In ancient Greece, Artemis was seen as the goddess of the hunt, as well as the protector of wildlife in general.

Up until the eighteenth century, a strange tradition was being carried out at the old St Paul's Cathedral, called the "Blowing of the Stag". Legend has it that the cathedral was built on the site of a Roman Temple of Diana (or Artemis) by the mythical King Brutus, who in legend gave his name to Britain. What can be said, however, is that a ceremony took place once a year on the Feast of the Conversion of St Paul on 25th January, and again on the Feast of the Commemoration of St Paul on 30th June. A report from 1598 describes the ceremony, stating that on the first occasion a doe, and on the second a buck, were given by the keepers and sheriffs of Hertfordshire and Essex to the Dean and Chapter, whose land they had purchased. The ceremony commenced when a keeper, wearing a tunic portraying a buck or doe on its breast, would lead the deer up to the high altar. Having been blessed, the deer was then slaughtered, its head cut off and fixed to the top of a pole to be displayed, and the body roasted as a feast for all concerned.

After this part of the ceremony was completed, a procession led the way out of the cathedral via the west door, with the deer's head (complete with antlers, in the case of the buck) at the front for all to see. Outside the doors, the keepers would blow long blasts on their horns to the four points of the compass, whilst more horn-blowers would do the same throughout the city to announce to the people of London that the ceremony was over. This event was also referred to as "The Hunter's Festival".[3] After the Great Fire of London in 1666, Christopher Wren's cathedral was built, and when construction commenced, a round Roman structure made of bricks was discovered under the previous building's foundations. And in 1830, digging work in Foster Lane northeast of the cathedral revealed a limestone altar dedicated to the goddess Diana, thus there is some evidence of a possible Dianic temple having been in the area. The stag of course was sacred to the goddess, and she was associated with the hunt.

Deer and their antlers feature in the folklore of many countries, and there are several tales from Irish and Scottish sources that include deer, which they call "fairy cattle", in which they are milked and herded by a supernatural woman who is able to shape-shift into a white or red deer. The Celts revered the stag, as it symbolised wild nature, its antlers imitating branches of trees.

It is apparent that the Anglo-Saxons regarded the stag as an important symbol of regal and political power. Indeed, Woden himself was described as being led to the abode of the Germanic goddess Holda by a stag, and it is recorded that he was also known as the stag himself. In Norse mythology, the fertility god Freyr is killed by a deer's antlers; and the stag Eikthyrnir that stood

---

3 *The Aquarian Guide to Legendary London*, edited by John Matthews and Chesca Potter (1990).

in Valhalla, the Viking otherworld, was known to cause cows to yield blood not milk, just as Herne himself was said to have done. In the Anglo-Saxon poem, *Beowulf*, there is a great feasting hall named Heorot, which translates as "Hall of the Hart", and in the great Anglo-Saxon ship burial of Sutton Hoo, archaeologists discovered a stone sceptre/whetstone mounted with the figure of a bronze stag complete with antlers. It is thought that the piece represented the power and authority of the King, who is thought to have been Raedwald of East Anglia, who hedged his bets by worshipping as a Christian as well as a pagan. Later, Richard II (he of the Herne legend) adopted the White Hart as his personal emblem, perhaps giving rise to the many inn signs up and down the country.

Moving on into Christian times, we encounter St Eustace, a Roman general who was martyred in 119 CE, on the orders of the Emperor Hadrian. He was converted to the new faith after seeing a shining cross between the antlers of a stag he was hunting, later being martyred for his faith. It was said of an English saint, St Tewdric, who led a hermit's existence near Tintern, that at his death his body was borne upon a funeral bier pulled by two stags. Ireland is the place where St Cainric received assistance from a stag, which used to hold a book in its antlers whilst he read; and a stag led another Irish saint, St Ciaran, to his future retreat upon an island in the middle of a lake.

An Arthurian figure, namely the wizard Merlin, also has connections with stags, like Cernunnos. An episode in Geoffrey of Monmouth's *Life of Merlin* (*Vita Merlini*), dating from 1150, features an event involving a stag. His wife Guendoloena decided she wanted to marry another, which made Merlin furious, and he got together a deer herd. He then mounted a stag and, along with the rest of the deer, he rode off to the wedding. Guendoloena saw the entourage, as did her bridegroom, who burst out laughing at the sight. It was then that Merlin caught sight of him and, realising who was, he straightaway tore off the antlers from his mount, whirled them around and hurled them at the bridegroom. This resulted in the latter's head being severely crushed, which caused him to expire. Having achieved his goal, Merlin turned the stag round and rode back to his abode in the forest.

The minions of the deceased bridegroom pursued him, but then he arrived at a river, and half way across Merlin fell off the stag. Having reached the other bank, the minions captured him and carried him to his sister Gwenddydd. The author Nikolai Tolstoy[4] firstly points out that it seems that Merlin had some sort of power over the deer, reminiscent of a pagan god. Secondly, he finds it bizarre the tearing off his mount's antlers, but he argues that in fact the antlers were Merlin's own, growing out of his head – but this is debatable. It shows, however, the prominence of the stag with its antlers in Britain's chronicles (and this author considers that it should be the emblem of the country, rather than the non-native lion).

Merlin in the guise of a deer meeting with Caesar
(Suite Vulgate, 1286)(Wikimedia Commons)

---

4 *The Quest for Merlin*, by Nikolai Tolstoy (1985), pp74–75.

In 1127, King David I of Scotland went out on a hunt and sighted a cantankerous white stag, which attacked him, injuring his thigh, and startled the King's horse, which ran off, leaving its rider lying on the ground. The stag stopped and glared at him, then he realised that he had lost both his bow and spear, leaving him vulnerable, as the animal charged at him with antlers lowered. It was then that the King saw a shining Holy Cross which had appeared between the stag's antlers, and when he grasped the Cross, the stag turned and dashed off into the forest. King David noted where this miracle took place and instructed that a church be built there, which evolved into an abbey, naming it Holy Rood or Cross. Eventually, another building was constructed adjacent to the abbey which became a guest house for royal visitors named Holy Rood House – now the seat of the Scottish Parliament. Along the Canongate section of Edinburgh's Royal Mile, images of the white stag with the Cross between its antlers can still be seen today.

Continuing this theme of trees and antlers, there is a curious tale from the Lake District which combines these two elements. The story goes that in 1333, Edward III was out hunting one day at Whinfell, Westmorland, when his hound Hercules took after a stag and chased it to Redkirks in Scotland and back. On their return, however, the stag had to leap over a fence, but died after it had done so. Hercules shared the same fate after he attempted, but failed, to clear the fence. Nearby stood an oak tree and, to commemorate the event, the stag's antlers were nailed upon it, whereupon it was known thence as the Hartshorn Tree. As with Herne's Oak, pieces from the tree seem to have been prized, as Lord Hothfield is reported as having such a piece on his writing table at Appleby Castle in 1922. Such is the magic of the oak.

DEER AND WINDSOR GREAT PARK

The stag, of course, plays an important part in the Herne legend, and stag hunting was always a royal pastime. Deer parks were first established in the days of the Anglo-Saxons, but after the arrival of the Normans the number of deer parks increased phenomenally. At first, the Norman kings kept the right to keep and hunt deer for themselves, but as the years went by, they permitted noblemen and high level clergy to maintain deer parks, and eventually they were popular with the country's upper classes. Henry I introduced strict laws of the forest, along with harsh punishments for those breaking them. For instance, if anyone killed a deer, the penalty was to be blinded.[5]

By the Second World War, the deer in the park numbered over 1,000 – mainly red deer and a smaller number of fallow and, as their browsing could interfere with food production in the park (needed for the war effort), it was decided that something had to be done. During 1940-41, 700 were culled and about 300 were kept in an enclosed compound with a high fence, covering about 300 acres. After the war, King George VI decided that, as rationing was to continue for some time yet and the country needed all the food it could produce, the remaining deer had to go to free the land. So, during 1950-51 they were transferred to Richmond Park, Badminton and Balmoral.

Thus, the park remained without deer until Prince Philip arranged for them to be returned in February, 1979, a herd of red deer being reintroduced from Balmoral, and they now number some 500. There are also a number of fallow deer, roe deer and a few muntjac. Berkshire has strong connections with deer, and Windsor Forest has been the haunt of these animals since time immemorial. One has only to look at Berkshire's emblem, a stag and oak tree, to realise the importance of deer to the area. Michael Petry goes further, however, and sees the royal county's emblem as harking back to Berkshire's origin when its name "oak-grove-shire" was a reference to Windsor itself. His theory was that the area around the mound upon which the Round Tower stands was an ancient, sacred place where an oak cult once

---

5 *Windsor Town and Castle*, by Henry Farrar (1990).

Windsor Park, with stags in the foreground, and the castle in the distance (1879) (Wikimedia Commons)

existed.[6] It is very probable therefore that the locality of Windsor Castle was sacred in prehistoric times, and may well have been a site which was favoured as a cult centre, perhaps once being the home of shamans bearing antlers upon their heads. Little is known about early Windsor before about 1070, but the chalk hill upon which the castle stands must have been prominent in the local landscape – a perfect place for a sacred gathering.

We have a long tradition of antlers' attraction to humankind, and their qualities seem to symbolise strength, fertility, new life and sexuality. That Herne should be said to bear a set of their "ragg'd horns" is no surprise, since the legend of Herne is reputed to haunt the area during the winter, and his death and return to life with the magical healing of Urswick can be seen to represent the "death" of the natural world during the winter period, only to be reborn in the spring.

Deer are again a common sight in the Great Park, and even if you are unlucky enough not to see any whilst walking through the park, you are certain to see the tracks they leave behind them.

6 *Herne the Hunter: A Berkshire Legend*, by Michael John Petry (1972), p22.

The rutting season, when the stags charge each other, engaging their antlers in battle, must have been a prelude to the arrival of winter's Wild Hunt led by Herne, who has adopted the stag's symbols of power and regeneration in his seasonal race through the forest and countryside of Berkshire. The calls of the stags can be heard echoing round the park, and there are those who claim that Herne's name is uttered by the red deer, and at dusk and dawn their braying is heard by some to sound like voices calling "Herne, Herne".

.

The Wild Hunt

"Still, still last the dreadful chase,
Till time itself shall have an end;
By day, they scour earth's cavern'd space,
At midnight's witching hour, ascend."

– Sir Walter Scott

Jacob Grimm, 1840
(Wikimedia Commons)

To begin this chapter, a little background to the origins of the phrase the "Wild Hunt", coined by the German folklorist Jacob Grimm (1785–1863), brother of Wilhelm Grimm – both of whom were responsible for gathering folk tales and publishing them in book-form, first in 1812 under the title *Grimms' Fairy Tales*, with many further editions being published over the years to come. Jacob was very interested in linguistics and delving into the origins of the German language, and he also contributed in what became the standard practice for the future study of folklore. The phrase the "Wilde Jagd" or "Wild Hunt" was first recorded by Jacob in his book, *Deutsche Mythologie* (*German Mythology*), published in 1835, which aimed to trace the mythology, folklore and superstitions of the ancient Teutonic race, from the earliest of times up until his day. In this tome, he brought the phrase into popular parlance.

Grimm argued that the Wild Hunt originated from pagan times, and the leader (mainly male but occasionally female) was a survival of folk beliefs surrounding the god Wotan, whose hunt was like that of an army going to war. He then went on to say that after Christianity came on the scene, the Wild Hunt morphed from a god-led solemn march into a host of devilish ghastly phantoms. Previously, the poet Felicia Hemans penned her poem *The Wild Huntsman* in 1823 (see appendix 3), which was based on German castles and Odenwald, a mountain range. As Ronald Hutton points out when describing Grimm's workings:

> "... *a general acceptance of two major points of Grimm's methodology: that ultimately the concept derives from ancient paganism and in particular from a cult of the dead; and that modern folklore can be used to patch up the gaps in the medieval and early modern record.*"[1]

The fact that Herne was a hunter confirms that his legend is, in part, a variant of the wider tradition termed the Wild Hunt (Folklore Motif E501). Common to most north European cultures, with parallels elsewhere in the world, Wild Hunt stories tell of a spectral hunt which courses across country, through forests and across the sky. It is usually led by some form of demonic personage, with an entourage of spectral horses, hounds, devils and otherworldly beings. This assemblage includes all manner of unfortunates, such as unbaptised children, suicides, murderers, adulterers, criminals, blasphemers, witches, as well as soldiers, clergy, courtesans and freemasons(!). They are often deformed or maimed, with their heads in their chests or facing backwards, or instead have deer's heads in the place of a human's. Others are

---

1 Hutton, p127.

missing heads, limbs and even have their entrails hanging out.

The Norse god Odin, cognate with the Saxon god Woden, was essentially a storm god manifesting himself in thunderous movement across the sky, mounted on his eight-legged horse Sleipnir, one of his nicknames being Atridr, which means Rider. In the case of Woden, whose name gives us Wednesday (Woden's Day), as well as a few place-names such as Woodnesborough in Kent (hill sacred to Woden), and Wednesbury in Staffordshire (Woden's fort). The god's name itself derives from an old Germanic root meaning furious, wild or mad, and it is appropriate for a figure who led his troops of dead warriors across the sky to Valhalla, where they engaged in eternal feasting and battling. It was in this respect that Woden earned the nickname Valfodr, meaning Father of the Slain. Just as Odin/Woden was accompanied by two ravens named Huginn and Muninn, so often did the hunters, the birds flying on ahead to see if anything dangerous was afoot.

Odin leading the Wild Hunt
(Public Domain)

During the autumn and winter period, Woden's worshippers, upon hearing the wind tearing through the forest, would say that the god was out riding with his band. The Saxons had a custom whereby they would leave the last sheaf of corn in the field to feed

Sleipnir. Herne was said to have gone mad before he committed suicide and, coupled with the wild nature of his hunts, there is more than a touch of similarity between him and the wildness of Woden. The passing overhead of Woden's Hunt was regarded as a portent of some disaster, as were many celestial events, such as the appearance of comets and eclipses. It was also believed that anyone who was unfortunate enough to see the Wild Hunt was likely to be carried off with them, cast to the ground, or be made blind or insane and, even worse, to speak to the Wild Huntsman himself meant certain death. The Huntsman was also known to throw down human flesh or even dead infants upon the unfortunate person unlucky enough to see him. Thus, here we see a parallel with the tradition of Herne, for it is said that a sighting of him heralds some national disaster, and his taking the cattle and making milk-cows yield blood tell of the fear that he, like Woden, instilled into people.

Variations of the Wild Hunt are found throughout continental Europe and the British Isles, and Herne's role is assumed by a variety of other characters, according to the locality of the story. For example, in France he is Charlemagne, Valdemar in Denmark, King Solomon in Spain, and in Germany Frederick the Great. In Wales he becomes Gwynn ap Nudd, Lord of the Dead, who inhabited the Celtic underworld Annwn, which legend places beneath Glastonbury Tor. It was here that he summoned the souls of the departed during his celestial flights. Gwynn is associated with another Welsh god of the underworld named Arawn, described in legend as a hunter who pursues a white stag in the company of a pack of hounds called the Cwn Annwn, or Hounds of Hell. White, with ears tipped red – they were regarded as harbingers of death.

In British mythology, these hounds are also known as Yeth Hounds, Yell Hounds, Wisht Hounds, Gabriel Hounds, Rachet Hounds and variations on these, and they were thought to be the souls of unbaptised children who flitted between heaven and earth. Their yelping sounds were probably thought to be the noise made by migrating barnacle geese as they flew overhead by night. Gabriel was the name given to the Hebrew angel who acted as psychopomp, or conductor of souls to the Christian heaven, and as such is similar to the Greek god Hermes, who guided souls to Hades.

A well-known figure from Britain was that of King Arthur, who leads the hunt at South Cadbury in Somerset, one of the places surmised to be the site of Camelot. The hill fort is said to contain a cavern wherein Arthur and his knights lie sleeping. At midnight on midsummer's day he is reputed to ride with his knights over the fort and down to a spring to quench the horses' thirst. There is also an ancient track nearby called Arthur's Lane or Hunting Causeway, where sounds of the hunt are heard during the winter months. Like Herne at Windsor, this is an instance of a particular figure leading the Wild Hunt at a specific site.

An historical personage reputed to lead the Hunt was a character named Wild Eadric, who held lands in the Welsh Marches in the eleventh century. In 1067, he led an uprising against the incoming Normans, and in 1069 he burnt down the town of Shrewsbury. It appears that he was never defeated in battle and eluded capture altogether; in fact he actually changed sides and joined King William in the invasion of Scotland in 1072. His death is not recorded, and tradition has it that he did not die at all, but had to suffer eternal punishment for changing sides by leading a Wild Hunt. It is said that, along with his fairy wife Godda and his band of followers, he races across country in a furious ride.

He always faces in the direction of the country with which England will be at war in the near future. His troop was seen just before the Crimean War in 1854, galloping past Minsterley in Shropshire. He was seen by a lead miner and his daughter, the latter disobeying her father's instruction to cover her face or she would go mad. She looked through her spread fingers to see Wild

Eadric as a dark man with flashing black eyes and curly black hair. He wore a short green cloak and a green cap with a feather in it. He also had a short sword and a horn. Ainsworth gives Herne a horn, and it seems that all Wild Huntsmen blow a horn to herald their arrival. Eadric was also sighted before the two world wars, and, in the summer of 1914, he appeared riding eastwards, and again in the summer of 1939. His warnings of war are similar to those Herne is reputed to give at the time of national disaster.

It was also said that if the Wild Hunt was hailed in good cheer, then the hailer would be rewarded, and as the Hunt went by, a horse's leg would be thrown down which, if kept to the following day, would transform into a nugget of gold. One is also immune from misfortune if one sees the Hunt whilst riding a horse shod with iron horseshoes.

An efficacious method of keeping the Wild Hunt at bay was to fix a pair of antlers or horns to the gables of one's house. If asked for salt or parsley, the Huntsman would gallop off without causing any harm; and other protections included standing on a white cloth, praying or holding a sprig of hazel, hawthorn or marjoram. Not everyone has the ability to see the Wild Hunt, however, but there is a tradition that children born at midnight have the privilege of seeing not only ghosts, but also the Wild Hunt. Other persons have automatic immunity, including good churchmen and honest herdsmen. There are even remedies for any misfortune which befalls anyone affected adversely, such as waiting one year when, on the Hunt's return, the evil will be undone.

The course of the hunt often follows a straight line, destroying anything in its path, and old Roman roads are a favourite highway. One such road is the Devil's Highway, which makes its way through Windsor Forest near Crowthorne, on its way from Staines (Pontibus) to Silchester (Calleva Atrebatum).[2] The arrival of the Wild Hunt is often presaged by the noise of wind

---

2 Petry, p45.

blowing through the trees, rattling chains, horses neighing, horns being blown and thunder. It often ends very suddenly with total silence, followed by a loud wind with the tops of the trees swaying, amongst other things. Oftentimes, the Hunt turns up during the twelve nights of Christmas, or at the summer solstice and the vernal and autumnal equinoxes.[3]

As Christianity took its hold upon the population of Britain, the pagan gods such as Woden lost their influence and were largely forgotten, except as figures in folk tales. And so Woden lost his role as Wild Huntsman, and other characters took his place, most commonly the Devil, who also bore horns. In Devon, we hear of a farmer returning from Widecombe Fair. As he climbed up a hill he reached a stone circle, when all of a sudden he heard the sound of a hunting horn and baying hounds. This was followed by a rider dressed in black and mounted on a black horse rushing past him, accompanied by his hounds. The farmer, emboldened by drink, called out "Hallow Old Nick! Show us some of your game!" – at which, the rider threw something to the farmer. After the Wild Hunt rode on into the night, the farmer found that he was holding the dead body of his own baby. He galloped home, only to find his wife in a distressed state saying that their baby had disappeared from its cot. Her husband told his wife what had happened to him, and showed her the still body of their deceased child.

Turning to Dartmoor, we come to the Dewerstone – a rocky crag named after Dewer, also known as the Wisht Huntsman, his name being derived from a Celtic word meaning the Devil. He is reported to terrorise Dartmoor at night in the company of his Wisht, or Yeth, Hounds, and he appears at the top of the Dewerstone as a figure dressed in black who holds a whip, whilst at the bottom sits a huge black dog. The tradition is that the Hunt, led by Dewer, would chase unfortunate souls up to the top of the highest crag and then vanish, leaving them to fall over the

---

3 Petry, p46.

edge to their deaths. Also said to lead the Wisht Hounds across Dartmoor is none other than Sir Francis Drake, who apparently was known to have an interest in the occult. He is reputed, on stormy and moonless nights, to drive a black hearse drawn by headless horses, accompanied by demons. The Dewerstone is the site of an Iron Age hill fort, and the name Wisht is a dialect word meaning "spooky" or "unearthly".

The capture of a soul is well illustrated by another tale, this time from Crowcombe in Somerset. Here an old woman was wending her way to market with her pony carrying her wares. Unfortunately, instead of setting out early in the morning, on this occasion she mistook the time and she left before midnight. After a while she fell asleep whilst on the pony, and when she awoke, she found the animal trembling with fear in a field. Then a terrified white rabbit hopped past her, and it was then she heard the baying of hounds. She felt sorry for the rabbit and let it hop into her pannier. However, the pony wouldn't move and she suddenly heard the sound of approaching hooves, and a black rider rode towards her and stopped.

The rider's horse had horns which shone with a green light, and the hounds breathed green fire. The black rider asked the old woman if she had seen a rabbit pass by, and when she shook her head, he led his hunt off into the night. It was then that the pony decided to move and galloped until they reached a ford, whereupon the old woman opened her pannier. It was no rabbit that emerged, but instead a beautiful lady who thanked the old woman for saving her. Apparently, she had been a witch when young, and, after she died, she was condemned to be hunted by the Devil and his Yeth Hounds, until she could get behind them, which the old woman had enabled her to do. At which the lady suddenly disappeared. This last story is of interest in that the horse had horns, and this is one of the few instances, apart from Herne, that features horns or antlers in connection with the Wild Hunt. It is therefore probable that an antlered figure was once a feature of the Wild Hunt throughout Britain, surviving only in the legend of Herne the Hunter of Windsor Forest.

Recorded in the Anglo-Saxon Chronicles, a well-known sighting of the Wild Hunt occurred at Peterborough in 1127. In that year, Henry I granted the abbacy of the town to one Henry of Poitou, which was an appointment unpopular with the local people. Immediately after his arrival, it was reported by many that they had both heard and seen huge, swarthy huntsmen riding on black horses and bucks. Their hounds were jet black and had horrible saucer-like eyes. They were observed in the local parklands and woods, and the monks heard their horns throughout the night, sounding like a couple of dozen or so horn blowers; with all this carrying on from Henry's arrival in February, and all through Lent, right up until Easter.

Herne the Hunter as Wild Huntsman is therefore a primeval symbol dating back to Palaeolithic times when life was harsher and dependent on the success of the hunt. This would have special significance during the winter period when food was scarce, and it is perhaps the wild, urgent chase that proved necessary at this time of year which ingrained itself into folk memory. That appears to be the reason why Woden and Herne are associated with midwinter. The uncertainty of obtaining food and of survival itself manifests itself in bringing of either good or bad tidings from Woden, and the warnings of national disaster from Herne. Herne's role as Wild Huntsman places him in a broader context, and the parallels described in this chapter reveal the extent of the idea of such a figure, recorded as he is from so many localities.

The cold, dark period of the year had its beginning in Celtic times with the festival of Samhain, the modern Hallowe'en. It was a time when the barriers between this world and the otherworld were let down and communication with the spirits was made possible. It was then that the hunter, in the guise of Woden, Gabriel or Herne, began his wanderings abroad to gather a spirit throng and guide them to their infernal abode. The "dead" time of the year was a period of fear and superstition, and it is not surprising that such ancient beliefs as we have come across in this chapter should all take place during the depths of winter. Thus, Herne's role as the Wild Huntsman and his affinity with Woden can be viewed against a wider background of folk belief, a figure recognised and feared across all of northern Europe. But as we have seen, this role is only one side of a more complex and composite character.

Connected to Woden is the folkloric character named King Herla, said to be one of the early British kings, and after whom the Wild Hunt is sometimes named, the whole form of Herla and his followers being known as the Herlathing. Herla and his troops used to wander the countryside in a never-ending march, and there is a record of a sighting one midday in 1154 in the Welsh Marches. Apparently, they were seen with horses, hounds, hawks and wagons; and when they were first sighted, the local people shouted and blew horns, whereupon the whole troop flew up into the air and vanished. There has been a suggestion of a connection between Herne and Herla by the similarity of their names. There may be a germ of truth here, but there is another link which is more interesting as it is relevant to perhaps the most important leader of the Wild Hunt, the Anglo-Saxon god Woden.

He was also known as Herian, which later became Herleke and was translated into Latin as Herlekinus. This again gave the French name Harlequin, and the Wild Hunt in France went under the name, amongst others, of La Mesnie Herlequin. The Harlequin which has survived as a figure into modern times at the festival of Carnival can be traced back to Herla. His costume as portrayed in the seventeenth century consisted of rags sewn together at random, which harked back to the rough garb of the Wild Huntsman himself. In some parts of France, however, St Hubert has taken Harlequin's place and at harvest time, as well as on St Hubert's feast day, the saint and his Wild Hunt are said to be heard. Nevertheless, in pre-Christian times, there is no doubt that Herian or Woden were to feature as an important hunt figure in folklore.

His name is to be found in folk tradition on mainland Europe and the Wild Hunt is led by him in the Netherlands (*Woedende Jager*) and Denmark (*Odinsjagt*); in the latter case, there is a Horn the Hunter, but he does not lead a Wild Hunt. Other names include *Wildes Gjoad* (Austria), *Wuetesheer* (Rhineland), and *Chasse Sauvage* (France). It is of interest to note that there is an ancient belief on the continent that the souls of the dead were ferried across the English Channel to Britain; and in north Germany the Wild Hunt is known as the *English Hunt*, probably because the sixth century historian Procopius recorded that the souls of the dead were conveyed over the English Channel to Britain.[4]

The baying and howling of the Hunts' hounds appear in the majority of the Wild Hunt accounts, most of them being black with red eyes and tongues, and they hunt packs or occasionally in single file. The Huntsman's horse can appear in a variety of colours, such as black, brown, russet or white. It also has red eyes and often breathes out flames like a dragon. As in the case of Woden, the Wild Huntsman was often accompanied by two ravens, which flew ahead warning him if there was any danger ahead, although an owl sometimes took on this task.

Herne's role as Wild Huntsman places him in a broader context, and the parallels described in this chapter reveal the extent of the idea of such a figure, recorded as he is in so many localities.

To finish this chapter, a more serious example of the Wild Hunt theme in the twentieth century, coming from the great psychologist, Carl Jung. A natural psychic, Jung had vivid dreams, and one in particular which he dreamt in November, 1922, is relevant here. It appears that on the night before his mother's death, he dreamt that he was in a dark jungle with huge

---

4 Petry, p44.

Carl Gustav Jung
(Ortsmuseum Zollikon, Wikimedia Commons)

boulders – a "primeval landscape", as he described it. All at once, he heard a piercing whistle which terrified him, but not so much as what appeared next. A gigantic wolfhound burst through the undergrowth with its jaws open and rushed past him. Jung knew instantly that it had been sent by the Wild Huntsman to take away a human soul. Jung woke up in terror and the next morning learned the news of his mother's passing. He thought that superficially the dream had meant that the Devil had come and taken her away, but a deeper interpretation gave the role to the Wild Huntsman. In his guise of Wotan, the god of his Alemannic forefathers had taken his mother to her ancestors – negatively to the "wild horde", but positively to the "saligLut", the blessed folk, concluding with:

"It was the Christian missionaries who made Wotan into a devil. In himself he is an important god – a Mercury or Hermes, as the Romans correctly realised, a nature spirit who returned to life again in the Merlin of the Grail legend and became, as the spiritus Mercuriliaris, the sought-after arcanum of the

110

alchemists. Thus the dream says that the soul of my mother was taken into that greater territory of the self which lies beyond the segment of Christian morality, taken into that wholeness of nature and spirit in which conflicts and contradictions are resolved."[5]

Works Consulted

The Witch, by Ronald Hutton (Yale University Press, 2018).

Memories, Dreams, Reflections, by C.G. Young (4th edition, Flamingo, October, 1987).

Herne the Hunter: A Berkshire Legend, by Michael John Petry (1972).

Additional Notes

1. See Appendix 3 for a poem on the Wild Huntsman.
2. It was said that if one placed a set of antlers above one's front door, you would be immune from the deadly Wild Hunt. I once visited the home of local Maidenhead historian, Michael Bayley (see *Encounters* chapter), and lo and behold he had a set of antlers on the front of his house above the door!
3. The verse quoted at the beginning of the chapter is from Walter Scott's poem, *The Chase*.

Black and white version of the image found on the front page of the Scottish chapbook, *Storys* [sic] *of the Wild Huntsman*
(Unknown author, *c*.1850, Wikimedia Commons)

---

5   Jung, pp344–345

Pagan Portals

PART ONE – CERNUNNOS

As described in the chapter *Origins*, there is a theory that the name of Herne the Hunter derives from the Celtic horned god Cernunnos, depictions of whom show him bearing two antlers, and in the example below also a torc hangs from each. Above the head appears the name Cernunnos in Roman letters, thus identifying the figure positively – though whether he was known by this name throughout the Celtic world is not known.

Cernunnos on the Pillar of the Boatmen
(Museum of the Middle Ages, Paris)
(ChrisO, Wikimedia Commons)

In ancient Gaul, Cernunnos as a cult figure is well attested, with a number of stone carvings showing a horned figure discovered in France, and elsewhere on the continent. His name is derived from the Celtic *karnon*, denoting horn or antler, which also appears in the name of the Gaulish tribe named the Carnutes (the horned ones). The earliest form of the French town of Chartres appears

112

around 400 CE as Carnotum, named after the tribe. The carving shown above is missing its lower half, which was probably portrayed as a sitting figure in a "Buddhist" pose.

The Celtic cult probably developed from horned gods worshipped in the Bronze Age or even earlier, and an example from Denmark illustrates this point. The figure takes the form of a rock carving portraying a horned god who, as well as being naked and phallic, bears a sword and holds a ship in one hand. This linking of phallic, horned figures with ships appears to be common in Bronze Age Denmark, and perhaps it represents the conveying of souls after death in a ship to the Underworld – as Charon ferries the dead across the River Styx in Greek mythology. The theme of guiding souls of the departed also appears in connection with the Wild Hunt (see chapter *The Wild Hunt*).

Cernunnos mosaic from Verulamium 160–190 CE
(Carola Raddato, Wikimedia Commons)

The cult of the horned god came to great prominence in the Celtic period and was overshadowed only by that of the head. It was well established in Britain before the arrival of the Romans, and certainly continued through the occupation period. Indeed, there is a fine example of a Roman mosaic in the Roman town of Verulamium at St Albans featuring the head of a god which was formerly seen as Oceanus, a marine deity, because of what were seen as lobster claws growing from his head. But this is now generally believed to be a variant of Cernunnos, and the claws are now considered to be antlers. Coming as it does from an important Roman town; it shows the prevalence of the idea of a horned deity in the British Isles (see illustration above p113).

The Cornavii, or People of the Horn, who lived in the area of Caithness in Scotland, may well have worshipped a horned god. Ptolemy, the second century CE Roman polymath, mentions their name in his *Geography*. It is also said that a deer goddess cult existed in the Scottish Highlands, and that they have always been regarded there as a supernatural animal, and fairy women were believed to be able to turn themselves into the form of a red deer.

The antlered goddess was also worshipped in Scotland based on reindeer, which were once native to Britain. Female reindeer have antlers, and there is a hamlet in Sutherland named Assynt – an Anglicisation of the Gaelic Innis nan Damh, which translates as "meadow of the stags".[1]

There is also evidence of a horned goddess cult in the form of a picture from a fragment of pottery found at Richborough in Kent, dating from the second century CE, showing the bust of a woman bearing horns. There were also tribes named Cornovii in the Midlands and in Cornwall, the latter being the area occupied by the Dumnonii tribe, perhaps revering Cernunnos. The late Dr Anne Ross suggested that in the case of the Midlands Cornovii, the Abbots Bromley Horn Dance had survived from pagan times, as the village is only 35 miles from the tribal centre of Viroconium Cornoviorum or Wroxeter (see also *Origins* chapter). It appears, though, that the three tribes of Cornovii had no connections each other, which is plausible as they are far apart from each other.

---

1 Chesca Potter interview at https://www.beliefnet.com/columnists/ dreamgates/2015/06/antlered-goddess-of-the-dreamways.html

The horned god was not always represented with stag's antlers, but sometimes with ram's or bull's horns, nevertheless they are all symbolic of power, vitality and fertility. Also connected with the latter in Celtic times is the image of the snake, whose habit of sloughing its skin was seen as a symbol of renewal. The most well-known example of the serpent together with Cernunnos is that to be found on the Gundestrup Cauldron discovered in the Danish district of Jutland in 1891, which had been purposely dismantled and deposited as a votive offering. It is made of silver and both the inner and outer faces are decorated with figures of gods and various cult scenes, the whole originally covered with a thin layer of gold.

Scene from the Gundestrup Cauldron, first/second century BCE
(National Museum of Denmark)
(Creative Commons Attribution-Share Alike 3.0 Unported)
(Wikimedia Commons)

The scene which concerns us, however, is that showing what appears to be Cernunnos bearing antlers sitting in a Buddhic pose, with a torc in his right hand and a ram-headed serpent in his left. He is surrounded by all manner of animals, but most prominent is the figure of the stag, its antlers almost touching those of the god. Here Cernunnos appears as "Lord of the Animals" – a trait he shared in common with the Greek god Hermes, who was the guardian of all animals of the land, sea and air, and thus presided over things of our earthly realm. This figure was considered amongst ancient hunters to be an entity that had power over wild nature and had to be propitiated to ensure successful hunting. Like Hermes and Pan, such figures were often depicted in half-human and half-animal guise.

The ram-headed serpent was not uncommonly associated with Cernunnos and was probably linked to the stag-god via the symbolism of the snake. As we have seen, antlers were regarded as symbols of fertility and sexuality, and the snake's phallic appearance, especially topped with a ram's head, is almost certainly due to its being that of another horned animal, and therefore is in sympathy with the antlered head of the god himself. Now there does not appear to be a direct connection with Herne, although Ainsworth did feature snakes in his novel when Herne made an appearance. But he was said to wield a chain in *The Merry Wives of Windsor* and, as mentioned earlier, it does not require much effort of imagination to see a development from a serpent to a chain.

As to other examples of Cernunnos figures in Britain, one stands out which was discovered at Petersfield in Hampshire. It takes the form of a silver coin depicting the only certain image of a deity from Celtic Britain. Dating from about 20 CE, it features the head of a bearded and moustached god with antlers, between which sits a crown surmounted by a sun-wheel. Another example emanates from Cirencester, the Roman town of Corinium. It portrays an antlered god in the normal squatting position, and on either side of his antlers are purses full of coins, or possibly cornucopias containing grapes, either way indicating fertility and plenty.

The image of a figure in chains was still extant in the medieval period and is shown in a carving to be found at Kirkby Stephen's parish church in Cumbria. Here we find a Viking portrayal of a horned figure bound in chains, named the Loki Stone[2] dated to the eighth century. It is a representation of the Norse trickster god, who is depicted chained to a rock until the Twilight of the Gods. It is obviously male and bears a set of ram's horns, but what makes it interesting is that both his arms and legs are bound together with a continuous chain. Thus we have a clear connection of a horned figure and chains. It is also significant that this figure dates from Viking times, for chains featured in rituals in honour of Odin/Woden. Tacitus tells of the Semnones, a Swabian tribe who would only enter a sacred grove to the god when bound in chains. These recurring concepts and personages turn up in different forms in a variety of cultures, and what we are seeing are variations on common themes.

The Loki Stone, Kirkby Stephen Church, Cumbria
(Annie Hamilton-Gibney, Wikimedia Commons)

The horned god is not only widespread and of ancient origin, but is especially prominent in Western Europe and Britain. It is likely that he was the Dis Pater, or Father of the Gods, whom Julius

2 In Viking mythology, Loki was a cunning figure who could change his shape and sex, and a companion of Odin and Thor.
   He is often portrayed as a scheming coward, mostly concerned with his own pleasure and his own self. He was responsible for causing trouble for the other gods, as well as humans, but he sometimes used his tricks for good purposes, and enjoyed making mischief.

Caesar identified as the ancestor of all the Gauls. However, the finer points of the cult of the horned god were to be lost with the arrival of Christianity, who transformed the figure into that of the Devil – that horned figure with bestial overtones. The image of the horns became associated with evil, and it was naturally assumed in the middle ages that witches worshipped a horned figure, as they were deemed to be in league with Satan. It then became the norm for all two-pronged objects to be associated with evil, for they represented the splitting of unity or God into two to create God an anti-God. Miranda Green, in her book, *Animals in Celtic Life and Myth* (1992), considers that "the protective character of the Celtic horned and antlered gods bears a far greater resemblance to the beneficence of Christ than to the image of the Devil." There is some evidence that pagan Celtic beliefs may well have lingered on into the Anglo-Saxon period, and the figure of the god could well have been kept alive in local Windsor folklore, who then morphed into Herne the Hunter, the leader of the Wild Hunt.

So, how far can we identify Herne with Cernunnos? The complex relationships of the multifarious themes within myths and legends from whatever culture or source is a subject which can provide clues and hints, and is itself a rich source of study. What can be said, however, is that Herne's story is set within a land which once revered the horned god to a considerable extent, this continuing well into Roman times. Perhaps it is not unreasonable to postulate vestiges surviving the coming of the Saxons and the merging of them with facets of Woden.[3]

Continuing with Woden/Odin, the voluntary death of Herne upon the old oak has so much in common with the Saxon/Viking god that it is worth investigating the parallel further. The two main and constant points in the variations on the Herne legend are: (a) he appears wearing antlers; and (b) he hanged himself

---

3 I use the name Woden rather than Odin, as the latter's stories are recorded, and it is probable that similar stories were told of Woden.

from a tree. This second point is of great significance in the quest for Herne's origins, as this ancient Norse piece relating the thoughts of Odin/Woden shows:

"I know that I hung on a wind-rocked tree,
nine whole nights,
with a spear wounded, and to Odin offered,
myself to myself;
on that tree, of which no one knows
from what root it springs.
Bread no one gave me, nor a horn of drink,
downward I peered,
to runes applied myself, wailing learnt them,
then fell down thence."[4]

These are the opening lines concerning Odin's self-sacrifice from *Havamal*, one of the *Verse Edda*, or ancient Icelandic poems, which are steeped in Northern mythology. *Havamal* means "the words of the High One" (i.e. Odin) and is a collection of verses in the form of charms and proverbs. The section which concerns us here tells how Odin hung from the World Ash, Yggdrasil, for nine days, how he was wounded by a spear, how he was given no food or drink, and how he grasped the runes and acquired a hidden knowledge. His spell hanging on the tree led to him to be known as Hangatyr, God of the Hanged, Galgatyr or Gallows God. It was the custom to make sacrifices to Odin, and stabbed victims were hanged from trees in the god's honour throughout the Germanic world. This practice was particularly carried out at the temple at Uppsala in Sweden, which continued until the tenth century. Enemy captives were strung up in honour of Odin and, in time of need, it may have been considered apposite to sacrifice a king, who was dedicated to the god. Thus Odin's experience on

---

4 Translation by Benjamin Thorpe (1782–1870), a scholar of Anglo-Saxon literature.

Yggdrasil was as a willing sacrifice in order to gain the knowledge he required, and this could be seen in a similar light to the action of Herne as he hanged himself on the oak tree. He had lost his woodcraft skills and also his job as a result. His solution was to sacrifice himself, to thereby regain his woodland knowledge, and thereafter he had successful hunting during those nocturnal rides through Windsor Forest.

Of course, the most well-known sacrifice in our own culture is that of Jesus Christ[5] who, like Woden, hanged from a tree, or more specifically a wooden cross. There has been speculation that the poem telling of Woden's sufferings was influenced by Christian teachings, but it is now generally agreed that Woden's fate emanates from an independent European tradition with its own primitive roots. Indeed, it can be pointed out that one of the reasons why the Jews ignored Christianity was, apart from being blasphemous, that it was claimed that Christ was divine. It also used a blatantly pagan concept of a god being killed for the good of his people and then being resurrected. The fact that this also occurred at Easter, when the pagan ceremonies of the spring rebirth and regeneration took place, only acted to confirm in the Jewish mind the paganism of this new faith.

The New Testament provides us with a further example of the sacrifice of a god-king in the person of Jesus. Whatever the interpretation of Jesus' life and death, he was certainly termed by the Romans as "King of the Jews", and the idea of the young god overcoming death and being restored to the land of the living to renew nature's life features strongly in the background of the Gospel story. As E.O. James puts it:

"In Christian tradition, this theme of the dying and reviving Year-god was brought into relation with that of the conquering

---

5 The term "Christ" is not a surname! It is the Greek word for the Jewish word "Messiah", meaning "the anointed one". So, as in the case of John the Baptist, whose epithet is obvious, Jesus (the Greek for the Jewish name Joshua) should strictly be referred to as Jesus the Christ.

Christ under the apocalyptic symbolism of the lamb slain sacrificially from the foundation of the world to ensure that final triumph of good over evil and of life over death." (Sacrifice and Sacrament, 1962)

Thus with Christ on the Cross, we arrive back again at Herne hanging from the oak – dying, perhaps, in place of his king, if the ancient underlying themes can be once more restored. In a sense, however, Herne died twice, for he was brought back to life by Urswick after being gored by the stag. But if the story can be read in this way, Herne's powers were not restored, but began to wane and there was therefore only one answer: self-sacrifice. This is thus very similar to Urswick in Herne's story, though the latter succeeded in his healing of Herne.

Returning to classical mythology, the myth of Heracles and his twelve labours brings us to the third – the capture of the Ceryneian Hind and bringing her back alive. The animal had brazen hooves and golden antlers, and was sacred to the goddess Artemis, and it took the hero Heracles a whole year for him to accomplish this labour. One version of the tale states that the hind was dedicated to Artemis by one of the Pleiades, to thank her for disguising her as a hind to avoid the amorous Zeus. Unfortunately, this did not work, and after her seduction she hanged herself.[6] This myth again features the themes of deer, sacrifices, hunting and hanging – so important in the legend of Herne.

Urswick is an intriguing figure in the legend of Herne and can be likened, perhaps, to characters such as Gandalf in Tolkien's *Lord of the Rings*, and to that Arthurian magician, Merlin. He is

---

6 The Pleiades, also known as the Seven Sisters, are a star cluster which feature in the mythology and folklore of many cultures. In Greek mythology, they are the companions of Artemis, the daughters of the sea nymph Pleione and Atlas the Titan. In Celtic mythology, they were associated with mourning the dead and funerals, with a festival at Samhain – which became Hallowe'en.

as mysterious as these characters, living alone as he does in his forest hut, and appearing out of nowhere at time of need. Indeed, he can be viewed as a shaman or even a Druid, both of which were healers amongst other things. As an oak cult survived well into Saxon times and the idea of a horned figure was still worshipped during the Roman period, it is not impossible that in Urswick we are seeing the shadows of pre-Christian Druidical priests who led a local cult in Windsor Forest.

Merlin bears many resemblances to the horned god, both of which having supernatural power over wild animals. Like Cernunnos, he was associated with certain animals, such as the wolf, pig and, most importantly, the stag. Now it may seem a strange and perhaps sickening act on Merlin's part to have torn off the stag's antlers at Guendoloena's planned wedding, but author Nikoloi Tolstoy suggests an explanation for this otherwise vicious act.[7] He surmises that it is not the stag's antlers that he removes so violently, but a set which, like Herne, he is wearing on his own head, and that the transfer to the stag occurred at an earlier stage of the tale through a misunderstanding (see also chapter *Stags and Antlers*).

However, there may be certain cases where a folk memory is carried over the centuries, and there is one that could be true. An excavation at Preseli in Wales by archaeologist Mike Parker Pearson has discovered the original stone holes which contained the bluestones at Stonehenge. There is an old tradition that Merlin brought the Stonehenge stones from Ireland and relocated them on Salisbury Plain. It seems that there is possibly a folk memory in action here, even though the stones came from Wales, not Ireland – but Wales is obviously well en route. Could this idea have worked in the case of Herne, his name morphed from {Cern}unnos over the centuries and become a local folk figure in the Windsor area?

---

7   *The Quest for Merlin*, by Nikolai Tolstoy (1985).

To conclude, Merlin, Cernunnos and Herne can be seen as aspects of the same figure – the Lord of the Animals, the dweller in the forest, the antlered one. They represent elemental, otherworldly beings that lord it over nature and lead a wild band – so much so that it has remained a part of our folk tradition in the form of Merlin and Herne. Tradition over the centuries has ultimately transformed them into a magician, the Devil, or some ghostly spirit. All in all, what remains is suggestive that the story of Herne the Hunter was that of the age-old theme of the annual cycle of the seasons and their importance to early man; but obviously this is speculation

PART TWO – NEO-PAGANISM

This section will be concerned with Herne the Hunter and modern paganism. I must state first that I shall be digging into the origins of how the horned god was embraced by the largely post-World War II pagan groups. There are a large number of pagan bodies in Britain, including Wiccans, Druids, Odinists, and just plain pagans (or Neo-Pagans), but I shall concentrate broadly on Neo-Paganism and Wicca.

To begin with, the connection with the figure related to Herne, the horned god, and the Green Man, only dates from 1939 when Lady Julia Raglan contributed her article "The Green Man in Church Architecture" to the *Folklore* journal in March of that year; prior to that, they were described as "foliate heads", and largely they were not taken much notice of. At the end of the article she concludes:

> *"The figure variously known as the Green Man, Jack-in-the Green, Robin Hood, the King of May and the Garland King … is the central figure in the May Day celebrations throughout Northern and Central Europe."*

Representation of a wicker man, from Aylett Sammes' *Britannia Antiqua Illustrata* 1676). http://www.joh.cam.ac.uk/library/special_collections/early_books/pix/whicker.htm (Wikimedia Commons)

As described above, examples of horned or antlered gods appear through the millennia and in various places. The modern pagan movement, largely influenced by the writings of Gerald Gardner and Margaret Murray, has flourished since the 1950s, and is now the fastest growing religious movement in Britain. Herne is a major figure/god in many of the branches of paganism, and is held by some to be a folk memory of the Celtic horned god, Cernunnos. There is a suggestion that the haunt of Herne, Windsor Forest, remained a Celtic stronghold for longer than the most of southern England, with the worship of Cernunnos lingering on into the later Saxon period and then merging with the Wild Hunt. Generally, Neo-Pagans and Wiccans accept the notion of a god and a goddess, a belief in the balance of male and female in the world; an idea largely lost, especially in the Western world, with the influence of the Abrahamic religions. It is a positive theme, which is gaining ground more and more, with Herne up there in the hierarchy of deities revered by the modern pagan community.

In his influential book, *The Meaning of Witchcraft* (1959), Gerald Gardner described Herne as a "British example *par excellence* of a surviving tradition of the Old God of the Witches." The idea of Herne/Cernunnos has been incorporated into pagan beliefs and rituals, and is as valid a god as any other. Artist and author, Chesca Potter, in her pamphlet, *Mysterious King's Cross* (1990), describes the stag-headed god as "The male fertilic power of nature, physically and spiritually. In prehistoric times, the shaman would have dressed in deerskins and a mask with stag-horns becoming as the god ..."

Herne the Hunter by Chesca Potter

Within the religion of Wicca, the horned god/Herne is seen as the consort of the Triple Goddess – a theme that is virtually absent from the main religions. She is a deity who possesses three aspects joined in one – consisting the Maiden, the Mother, and the Crone – representing the individual stages in a woman's life; her consort being the male horned god. These concepts were propounded by the poet, mythologist, Classicist, and novelist, Robert Graves, whose ideas were eagerly taken up by Neo-Pagans and Wiccans especially in his *The Greek Myths* (1955 and later editions) and *The White Goddess* (1948 and later editions). Again, though, such themes are not accepted by modern mythologists and students of ancient religions. Margaret Atwood, however, read *The White Goddess* at the age of 19, and found that the concept of the Triple Goddess used "violent and misandric" imagery. Her novel, *Lady Oracle* (1976), has been seen as a parody of the Triple Goddess.

The modern pagan movement has flourished since the 1950s, and is now the fastest growing religion in Britain. Herne is a major figure/god in a number of the branches of paganism, and is held by many to be a folk memory of the Celtic horned god, Cernunnos. This idea of Herne/Cernunnos has been incorporated into pagan beliefs and rituals, and is as valid a god as any other.

The horned god is seen as an ancient fertility god, presiding over fields and forests and, of course, the hunt. He is the lord of life, death and resurrection, the hunter and the hunted, as well as the protector of the goddess. Along with the Green Man, they are the chief male figures that feature in much of modern paganism, representing the spirit of nature, with Herne being particularly associated with hunting and presiding over the living world. His antlers on his head represent the bond between the concept of the divine and that of the human and animal world.

Nowadays, pagans often see him as a solar god connected with the trees and plants – the Oak King, when he is considered to be a fertility god, with his antlers symbolising energy and vigour – and Herne is also known as Keeper or Lord of the Forest. The Oak King and Holly King battle it out annually, which represents the seasons as they change over the year. At midsummer, the Oak King is at the peak of his power; the Holly King similarly at midwinter. In Wicca, Herne is seen as Lord of the Underworld as well as Lord of Life, his symbol being the sun, ruling over the dark winter months; the goddess ruling over those of summer. Herne is also a god of fertility, portrayed sometimes as ithyphallic, looking over the fertility of animals which people needed to hunt.

Of course, Herne's rule over the winter period also extends to that over humankind. Belief traditions in a number of Wiccan groups see the horned god as dual features of the Oak King and the Holly King. The medieval poem *Sir Gawain and the Green Knight* and the Celtic legend of Lugh and Balor could be read as an echo of this ancient battle, but that is debatable. The Wild Hunt is also an element in certain pagan groups, and in Wicca; and the leader of the Hunt is the goddess Hecate, the Greek goddess concerned with witchcraft, the moon, and sorcery. Neo-Pagans see her as the goddess of crossroads and mediator between realms. Again, these views are not accepted by historians, but they are seen by pagans as a valid base for their belief systems.

Hecate
(British Museum, Wikimedia Commons)

Now for two relevant quotes, firstly from Nicholas R. Mann, in his book, *The Keltic Power Symbols* (1987):

> *"The God, the Horned God, Herne the Hunter, the Green Man of the Forest, the Lord of the Animals, the Wild Man, the God who dies and rises with the year … The God who is the Hunter – Herne, Kerne, Kernnunos – becomes the prey he hunts … And through the transformation of spirit into the soul living beings the man knows the secrets of life and death, the unity of the whole, and he willingly goes into the Underworld to become the God of the Earth. He is the Star Son, and the Serpent Son growing and dying with the year … Together, the God and the Goddess are the Great Round of the earth, of the seasons, of Daily Life. And through the sharing of knowledge of the common source of life, immanent, immediate, all worlds become open, and the common journey with the other inhabitants of the Planet begins."*

And secondly, Joan Forman in her 1989 book, *The Haunted South* (p203), makes the following reflection:

> *"Herne is actually of ancient lineage … he was the horned god of primitive man, maybe Palaeolithic in origin, an incarnation of the animal to be hunted, a representation of a nature spirit. So this pagan god survived into medieval times, when he was regarded by the Church as a devil. [He] survives still into modern times when he is called a ghost, a supernatural spirit. Yet in honest fact, those who see Herne in the twentieth century are probably calling up a racial memory or an archetypal image of what was once an object of reverence and religious meaning to the northern races … What he is not, I think, is the ghost of a Plantagenet verderer who hanged himself from a forest oak. Cernunnos, the Celtic god of the underworld, he just*

might be, with a grove once sacred to his worship in the ancient park. But older still I think he is, belonging to the days when all men were hunters and all deer their quarry; the horned god, the god of the hunt."

I hope that I have given a positive and faithful account on modern pagan beliefs. Having taken this in, I end this section with two instances where Neo-Pagan beliefs concerning Herne and his reverence have been thwarted by twenty-first century ignorance and intolerance, as these two examples demonstrate:

(1) Herne Refusal in Wendover, Buckinghamshire:

In 2016, a sculptor, whose name I could not discover, suggested to Wendover Parish Council that he (she?) sculpt a statue of Herne for placement at Hampden Pond in Wendover, Buckinghamshire, where he himself lived. The Council proceeded to arrange a questionnaire on the proposal sent to the local residents. The objective was to "enhance the visual experience of visitors and walkers," with the proposal of the installation of a piece of sculpture on Hampden Pond Island.

The sculptor was an experienced artist, and his work had been sold in private collections in the UK and around the world. He was enchanted by Hampden Pond with its withered charm and that it had a wonderful ancientness about it, what with the exposed white craggy, gnarled root systems of the trees on the island. He added that it was the perfect location for his favourite sculpture to date – Herne the Hunter. His sculpture would be gazing upwards and his demeanour would complement the serenity and peace of the pond. He saw the sculpture of Herne as less of a hunter and more of a woodland deity. The figure's surface has woodland leaf cut-outs all over, making him almost see-through in a sense – so much so that he is almost camouflaged in the foliage of summer and the bare branches of winter. The artist envisaged that the sculpture could become a landmark for walkers, children and teachers, and pointed out that the Wendover section of the Ridgeway National Trail route came close, and a plaque on the walkway would tell his story.

The outcome was that the plan was rejected by Wendover Parish Council for whatever reason, and as the sculptor could not be identified, unfortunately I have to leave things here – a worthy project sadly unfulfilled.[8]

(2) Herne Refusal in Scotland:

Again in 2016, a pagan named Andrew Cleghorn living in Scotland wished to construct a tribute to Herne the Hunter on his eight acre smallholding near the village of Cardrona. His plan included an altar, a sacred well, and a plinth for a statue of Herne, as part of an application which included the erection of a two-storey building for the cold storage of rare-breed poultry. Enabling the plans to go ahead entailed obtaining planning permission from the local council, the Scottish Borders Council. At the following council meeting, Cleghorn outlined his plan which was "guided by the pagan earth gods and wishes to create a special place for private worship ..." adding that "the low-impact sacred well and altar/statue stance will be sited at the source of a spring on the hill, with a clear view over the valley ... where private meditation and worship can be carried out without impact to others." In addition, he wanted a cattle flotation pool for swimming therapy for the tonal improvement of the livestock (one caustic councillor commented that cows were not that keen on swimming).

Cleghorn's submission was rejected by the Council; the planning officer stating that he had no economic reason for the plans, and that it would compromise the character of the landscape and its proximity to the protected landscape of the

---

8 *Wendover News*, 21st October, 2016.

Tweed Valley. He was also told that his "extravagant" plans for a statue of Herne might cause upset to neighbours, as well as to the congregation of a nearby church.

Cleghorn was angry at this decision, stating that he was being persecuted by being prevented from following his spiritual beliefs, both in his home as well as at his smallholding.[9]

It was a shame that the above two statues did not come to fruition, the second case most likely through religious ignorance and bigotry, and it was probably the same reason in the first instance. It is a terrible thought that such uninformed attitudes and lack of understanding are still rife today. However, the spirit of Herne the Hunter is thriving – and long may it be so.

PART THREE – WICCAN HERNE

In magical working, it is apparently useful to know that Herne's sign is Taurus the Bull, his colour is green, and his emblems are a bow, a white stag and the moon. During meditation, Herne is not easily invoked – a hunter figure only normally appears when one is spiritually troubled, or was a hunter in a previous incarnation. In pagan circles, Herne epitomises the life-force and rules over the cycles of life, death and rebirth; and covens' ceremonies often reflect these attributes. Indeed, the preferred ritual headgear of the high priest is often the horned crown.

Within the religion of Wicca, the horned god, often equated with Herne, is seen as the consort of the Triple Goddess – a theme that is virtually absent from the main religions. A Wiccan priestess, Rowan Morgana, on her website starts off her section on the horned god thus:

"Who is this wild God who roams the forests, and who loves and protects the Goddess and all her children? He is called the

9 *The Scotsman*, 22nd September + 5th October, 2016; and *Peebleshire News*, 22nd September, 2016.

God of the Wicca, Cernunnos, Pan, Herne, Dionysus and by
many other names. He is the ancient God of fertility: the God
of forest, flock and field and also of the hunt. He is Lord of Life
and He gives life, He is also Lord of Death and Resurrection. He
is the hunter and the hunted, he is the light and the darkness."

Here I quote a chant used at the festival of Samhain, by Wiccan
the late Rhiannon Ryall, from her book, *West Country Wicca: A*
Journal of the Old Religion, published by Capall Bann in 1989.
She describes a chant used at the festival of Samhain. Moving
clockwise round the ritual circle, the men chant the following
rhyme:

"Iron clad the meadows,
Hoar frost covers all.
Weasel slithers whitely,
Black rocks give call for call,
Fox shadows on the hillside,
Hunters Moon it swings on high,
The Wild Hunt is out now,
Winds through the chimney's sigh.
Herne comes awalking,
While the Lady takes her rest.
Loving, warm and gentle,
White dove within her nest.
Herne comes astriding,
On Dolmen, Tor and hill,
Sees the hunter and the hunted,
In sky and field and rill.
Herne he comes aleaping,
His Kingdom hard and cold,
But all are his own ones,
The frightened, shy or bold.
Herne he does his making,

His minding and his sending,
He cares for all in this Realm,
And in the next one tending.
Death is but a doorway,
Herne is on both sides,
Here or there don't matter,
Old Herne with us abides."

The passing of his spirit into the soul of other beings, like a stag, enables the hunting god to acquire the secrets of life and death. Together, the god and goddess represent the cycle of the seasons and the sharing of life itself with the rest of creation – an idea which is echoed in the philosophy of the Green movement. The god and goddess complement each other and symbolise the partnership that is required for a balance and harmonious existence on this planet. A fitting exposition to end this chapter I feel.

Wiccan God, Goddess and Son of the Sun
(Camocon, Wikimedia Commons)

Encounters

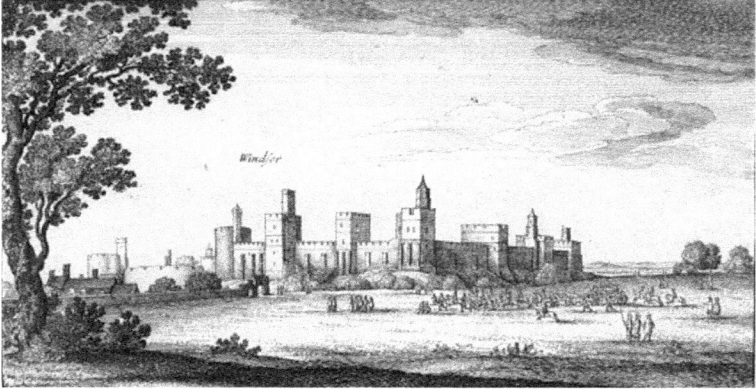

Windsor Castle by Wenceslaus Hollar in 1644
(Wikimedia Commons)

GHOSTS

Traditionally, ghosts have been regarded as spirits of the dead, especially of those who met an unfortunate end involving such dramatic events as murders and suicides. It appears that such spirits, however their actual nature is defined, are earthbound and remain at the spot that the original event occurred. Another explanation is known as the "stone tape" theory, which involves a traumatic event "imprinting" itself on its immediate surroundings, usually (but not always) a building, and being "played back" under certain circumstances.

There is much to commend T.C. Lethbridge's theory of "psyche fields", which involve the thought-forms of one individual becoming impressed into the static field of, say a building, tree or other place, and then being picked up at some future date by third parties. Alternatively, manifestations may occur as a result of telepathic communication, either by the person who is experiencing an event acting as a transmitter, or by someone observing that event. Often, though, ghosts of whatever type are seen only by psychics who are attuned to wavelengths closed to many of us. Is, therefore, Herne a ghost or some other manifestation?

ROYAL WINDSOR GHOSTS

Windsor Castle has a fair number of ghosts. Beginning with Henry VIII, he is reputed to haunt the cloisters near the Deanery, groaning with the sound of his dragging footsteps (he had suffered a bad leg which caused him to be in great pain). His second wife, Anne Boleyn, he had beheaded at the Tower of London, but she is said also to haunt the Dean's Cloister, where she sadly stares out of a window. Queen Elizabeth I reputedly haunts the Royal Library, and Charles I haunts the Canon's House. Moving on to George III, he has been seen looking through the castle's doors and windows, with a mournful look on his face, muttering "What? What?" (which he used to say in his old age). Interestingly, when the king died and was lying in state, the Castle Guard carried out its usual march past the royal chambers; the commander automatically looked up to see the old king. He then gave the "eyes right" order, and the guards obeyed, seeing the deceased king responding at his customary window. In 1936, local workmen stated that they saw Queen Victoria's ghost walking from the castle towards them, whilst waving her arms about as well as noisily moaning. But the ghost that is the most well-known is none other than Herne the Hunter who, although not being a "Royal" himself, had plenty of royal connections.

HERNE THE HUNTER

The spectral appearances of Herne the Hunter have much in common with other ghostly manifestations; the chief difference, of course, being that of the antlers. There are wild hunts recorded in many areas of Britain and abroad, and ghosts wielding chains are a common feature of traditional phantoms – however, Herne is no ordinary ghost. The writer on British spectres, Joan Forman, analysed and arranged supernatural apparitions into ten categories; and Herne the Hunter falls into that which she describes as a "primitive, archaic or racial memory manifestation." Examples of this type include such spectres as the phantom dog Black Shuck in East Anglia, and the Wild Hunt led by whoever the local huntsman happens to be. These types of ghost represent a deep, unconscious memory of the past and its history or even prehistory, and thus question whether modern humankind has really cut itself off from its roots.

Herne's appearances also overlap somewhat with another of Forman's categorisations, i.e. the "single event" where a dramatic event took place – in this instance, Herne's suicide. In this case, however, we have a ghost whose appearances do not fit exactly into any category, since he is traditionally said to appear during the winter months; but in more recent times has heralded times of national crisis, irrespective of the time of year. Herne's suicide also has much in common with that of another figure associated with Windsor Great Park. At Snow Hill, at the southern end of the Long Walk created by Charles II, stands the Copper Horse, a statue depicting George III (remember him?) on horseback, sculpted by Sir Richard Westmacott in 1831. The story (which I recall, having been brought up in Windsor) goes that Westmacott killed himself in disgrace because he had omitted to place one of the stirrups on the statue. Afterwards he was said to haunt the Long Walk; but if one visits the statue, neither stirrup is there, as the King was portrayed in the likeness of Roman cavalrymen, who did not wear stirrups. In reality, Westmacott lived until the ripe old age of 81.

Which brings us to Herne's sightings. Although in the past Herne has been used by parents as a bogeyman to scare and control their children, the number of authenticated cases of encounters with him are few and far between. Beginning again with Joan Forman, in her 1987 book, *Haunted Royal Houses*, she recorded that a member of the Royal Family confided to her that Herne had been seen sometime during the twentieth century. Thus, insubstantial though some reports may be, we have here a royal assent as to sightings, wherever, whenever and, most of all, which royal figure(s) did he appear to.

We start with the author Hector Bolitho, who tells of an encounter in his book, *The Romance of Windsor Castle* (1946). One passage relates the story of a man whom he met once walking through the Great Park who told him that when he was a schoolboy at Eton, he heard the sound of Herne's horn and hounds. It is difficult to pinpoint exactly when this happened, but perhaps we could guess at a date in the first decade of the twentieth century. Shortly after, the Hon. Evan Baillie, a Scottish merchant, landowner, slave-trader and onetime Whig MP, is reputed to have had a "close encounter" of a kind when he too heard Herne's horn and hounds. Unfortunately, these are the only details we have, and his son Lord Burton was asked about his father and Herne, but was unable to provide any further information. In his book, *The Quest for Merlin*, published in 1985, Nikolai Tolstoy tells of his friend, the poet Charles Richard Cammell, who was also once an Eton schoolboy before the First World War, who told him of an old keeper he knew. Cammell often conversed with this man, who claimed to have seen Herne on his wild chase. These encounters are rather nebulous, but later sightings are a bit more concrete, as long as one believes their accounts.

Another sighting of Herne is recorded in *A Dictionary of Fairies* (1976) by the renowned folklorist and onetime President of the Folklore Society, Katharine Briggs. Here she recalls that in 1915, whilst she attended a school in Edinburgh, one of her teachers related that her father, who was a retired colonel living in apartments at Windsor Castle, often saw Herne on moonlit nights under the branches of Herne's Oak, which I surmise must have been Victoria's tree which blew down in 1863.

Herne's hounds have been heard over a wide area, from Winkfield, where the Herne's Oak pub was situated, through Windsor to Old Windsor, and it is at the latter place that the next story takes place. An account from a Justice of the Peace and a member of the Windsor Board of Guardians, a certain Mrs William Legge[1] of Farm House, who was considered to be a level headed person, who had two encounters with Herne in 1926. On the first occasion, she had just retired to bed one night when she heard the baying of hounds which appeared to come from the direction of Smith's Lawn,[2] the sound getting louder until it died away in the direction of the castle. At that time of night, it could only be Herne's hounds.

Almost two weeks later, she heard them again, this time at precisely midnight, and, on this occasion, she was not alone, for her daughter too heard what she described as "strange sounds, almost like Herne the Hunter's hounds." Mother and daughter had just returned from London and were standing outside the house briefly before retiring. This time it appears that they heard the hounds travel towards the Copper Horse from the direction of Bear's Rails, an area within the Great Park which was once a site of bear-baiting, which has been a Boy Scouts' camp[3] for some time. Mrs Legge and daughter lived at Farm House for many years

1 This was in the days when married women would be referred to in any kind of document by their husband's first name.
2 A polo ground where Prince Philip and Prince Charles played.
3 This author remembers a weekend camp there when he was a Cub Scout.

afterwards, but never again heard the ghostly hounds. What is convincing about these two reports is the time, for who would be hunting so late at night but Herne? Angus MacNaghten, author of *Haunted Berkshire*, published in 1986, who knew Mrs Legge, asked her grandson if he could elaborate on his grandmother's account. Although he was a schoolboy at that time, he was aware of the story, as he well remembered her talking about it. He added that the two ladies were adamant that the hounds were certainly not a "tangible pack", as it was around midnight or 1am when they heard it. Mrs Legge was probably more believed, being a J.P. and a "trustworthy citizen".

The next encounter, again from the 1920s, provides us with the only detailed sighting of what can only be Herne the Hunter, if you take it to be true. This took place at Cookham Dean, which used to be at the edge of Windsor Forest in times gone by, as the Forest extended over much of east Berkshire, south Buckinghamshire and northwest Surrey. It was a summer's evening when another highly regarded woman was crossing the local common on her way back from posting a letter. Part way across the common, she became aware that her two dogs appeared to be frightened, and instead of running on ahead, they cowered behind her. It was then that she saw a man emerge from the undergrowth surrounding an oak tree, but it was no ordinary man, for on his head he wore a set of antlers. She was not afraid, however, and instead of continuing on her way, she decided to follow the figure, which crossed the common, whereupon it disappeared. This account is significant in two respects, the first being its importance as an authentic Herne sighting. The second reason is the site where he disappeared, that being at an oak tree which, as we have already seen, is highly relevant when discussing Herne. All in all a fascinating encounter.

Moving on to the 1930s, there were apparently a number of sightings made during this decade, including one made by some workmen who were engaged upon renovations at the castle – although I consider this account to be rather tenuous. Could this be the workmen having a laugh? A bit more plausible is the sighting by a local woman who claimed that she heard and saw Herne's hounds run across an open space in the Great Park on one bright moonlit night. On another occasion, which occurred in 1936, two Eton schoolboys claimed they heard an invisible hunt in full cry galloping towards them. Although they did not actually see anything, they reported that they experienced an icy blow as the unseen hunt rushed past them.

And now a 1940s sighting made by another schoolboy on his way from his home in Englefield Green to his school in Windsor on a misty autumn morning. This was during the Second World War when the deer had been removed from the Great Park. His route by bicycle took him down the Long Walk towards the castle, when he suddenly caught sight of a person wearing a set of antlers sitting on a horse, silhouetted against the murky mist. His view was only a momentary glimpse, but it was enough to have turned his knees to jelly!

The Long Walk from the top of Snow Hill
(William Gauci, c. 1827, British Museum)

We now arrive at the 1960s, with two versions of the same tale, which has been described as an updating of an ancient folkloric theme and is probably the most well-known encounter. The action was said to have occurred in 1962, and involved a group of three youths who were mucking around in the Great Park one night. They came across a hunting horn and, at the edge of a clearing, one of them picked it up and blew it. To their surprise there was an answer from another distant horn, followed by the sound of hounds coming towards them. Shortly after, Herne himself appeared mounted on a black horse, at which the terrified youths dropped the horn and ran for their lives.

And now for the full story, known as Herne's Horn, which can be found in a 1970 book by Ruth L. Tongue.[4] The story, which ends in tragedy, involves two youths from Windsor and a Teddy Boy.[5] On this particular day the three of them went out into the Great Park, obviously up to no good, spending their time breaking down young trees. The Teddy Boy, however, suddenly stopped and picked up what looked like a hunting horn, and shouted out to the other two what he had discovered, wondering if it was a prop from a Robin Hood film. However, the other two looked at him a bit oddly, and the Teddy Boy came over a little uneasy himself, as he realised that it was highly improbable that filming in that environment could have taken place with bushes all around. Immediately, the two Windsor youths frantically shouted out to him to leave it alone and dashed off as quickly as they could.

---

4 *Forgotten Folk-Tales of the English Counties*, edited by Ruth L. Tongue (1970). The tale was told in 1964 at Cecil Sharp House by a Berkshire Morris member of the English Folk Dance and Song Society.

5 Teddy Boys, or Teds, were the first of the post-war youth movements, starting in the early 1950s. They dressed in clothes mimicking those worn in the Edwardian period, as well as black suede creepers; the Teddy Girls choosing to dress in pencil skirts, drape jackets, and rolled-up jeans. They listened to rock'n'roll, skiffle, and rhythm and blues (or R & B), but the sub-culture largely died out come the Mods and Rockers in the early 1960s.

Nevertheless, bravado overcame over the Teddy Boy and he blew it – the horn emitting a groan and a resounding boom, resulting in him nearly fainting and beginning to shake all over. Then suddenly all three heard a terrifying yell along with the baying of mighty hounds coming from the nearby trees, with the Teddy Boy quickly deciding to follow his mates. However, he could not keep up with the others, who were running flat out towards a church,[6] and he stumbled and shivered as he could hear the sounds of the hunt following him. The Windsor youths finally made it to the safety of the church, turning to see their friend struggling on, with the sound of the hounds still baying. The Teddy Boy arrived just in front of the church door, when the "hunter" stopped. Then they all heard the sound of an arrow flying through the air, and the Teddy Boy threw up his arms, screamed and fell down dead in the church porch. But the two Windsor boys saw no sign of the hunter, his hounds, nor an arrow in their mate's body.[7] A frightening episode indeed.

It is no surprise that soldiers guarding the castle have been recorded knowing that it had been haunted for hundreds of years. When they thought they sighted Herne, it was said that they would quickly tell the locals, for his appearance was said to bring death to their cattle, as well as blight crops and trees. To begin with, an account concerns a young recruit of the Grenadier Guards whose ghost haunts the Long Walk. According to the legend, he is said to have shot himself because he saw Herne, but presumably he had time to tell someone about his encounter before he expired. A few weeks later, his ghost was seen by a guardsman on duty, who saw the figure of his dead colleague

6 I have looked into the matter of the nearest church with a porch to the Great Park, and have come up with Windsor Parish Church of St John the Baptist, or the Old Windsor Parish Church of St Peter and St Andrew. The former is in Windsor High Street – which is unlikely as it's in the town centre, and the latter is a bit too far south of the Great Park. So, I assume that in this case the church must be due to imaginative fabrication.
7 For folklorists, this account is a variation on the Folklore Motif E501 – The Wild Hunt.

in the bright moonlight. When he returned to the barracks, he discovered that the sentry he had previously relieved had experienced a very similar encounter.

The Coldstream Guards now appear on the scene with another guardsman who was on duty at the East Terrace of the castle near the State Apartments on September 22nd, 1976. It is said that he was found unconscious by his relief, who could not bring him round. After he was taken to the barracks' medical block, he eventually regained consciousness and he told of a strange apparition he had witnessed. He informed his adjutant that he had been performing his guard duty as normal, when his eyes fell upon one of the statues in the Italian Garden. His recollection was that, as he looked at it, the statue began to grow horns and suddenly came to life, after which he fainted (whether the horns were antlers is not stated). After his experience, he was allowed a few days' rest to recuperate in hospital, and latterly he declined to comment on his incident, despite requests made via his battalion.

Buckingham Palace have stated that they had never heard of a ghost of any kind at the castle, and dismiss the report altogether. This is strange, considering that a number of ghosts are said to haunt the castle, as mentioned at the beginning of this chapter.

Windsor Castle, East Terrace, 1890
(Wikimedia Commons)

However, the story was reported in the *Windsor Express* on 1st October, and a lady reader contacted the newspaper saying that it was amazing that they had never heard of Herne the Hunter. She was convinced that it was Herne who had materialised: "… this guardsman, poor devil, might have seen something … he might be in trouble." She added that her grandmother had told her 60 years previous of Herne sightings. The story she related was that Herne himself had a daughter who was seduced by Henry VIII, which drove her mad. A spokesman at Windsor's Victoria Barracks announced that there would be no charge against the sentry on guard on the East Terrace. However, local folklore claims that the sentry never recovered from his terrifying experience, and it is said that he became a gibbering wreck, unable to come to terms with what he saw.[8] The East Terrace is especially prone to hauntings, and an incident from the nineteenth century involved another guardsman. On duty one night, he saw a strange creature resembling an elephant and, being very frightened, he shot at it. The bullet went straight through the apparition, which suddenly vanished.

A castle historian pointed out, however, that Herne himself has never been seen at the castle itself, but only in the forest. He also recalled a not unrelated tale. One cold winter's night many years ago, a young soldier was standing guard at the castle, and it seems that the Dean of Windsor took pity on him and brought a bowl of gruel to warm him up. Unfortunately, when the guardsman saw a cloaked figure approaching him, he panicked and fired his gun, just missing the poor clergyman. His punishment was twenty lashes.

A more recent experience of Herne was a BBC broadcast in 2015, dealing with the folklore of Britain – one episode of which was devoted to Herne the Hunter. During the programme, there was a brief interview with a warden of Windsor Great Park, who

---

8   This account was told to me personally by a local Windsor policeman, *c.*1992.

told of his encounter with Herne. He and a couple of friends were doing some late night fishing at Russell's Pond in the park, when they heard the sound of a galloping horse emanating from a nearby copse. They immediately formed an opinion that it was the sound of a hunt, but who would be hunting in the middle of the night? – It must be Herne the Hunter.[9]

Returning to royalty, the shouts of the Wild Huntsman were heard as he rode across the sky on the eve of Henry IV's murder in 1413. Whether it was Herne himself is not possible to say, but Henry IV was the man who ordered the killing of Richard II, who was haunted by Herne. Perhaps it was the first sighting of Herne after the demise of Richard, for it was not to be until he died that Herne would resume his haunting.

Coming up to more modern times, there have been a number of sightings which occurred just before a crisis in Britain.[10] He was seen just before the General Strike in 1926, and was said to have appeared just before the Depression in 1931, when he materialised along with a white stag and the ghostly form of his oak. He reappeared before the abdication of Edward VIII in 1936, the outbreak of the Second World War in 1939, and the death of George VI on 6th February, 1952. In the latter instance, an observer recorded that when he was walking along Windsor High Street on that day, he heard the Sebastopol Bell ringing in the Round Tower, which only occurs when a royal death is imminent. The news of the king's decease had just been received, and the remarks of a passing woman were worth reporting. She was heard to say: "I knew some dreadful tragedy had happened, for Herne the Hunter was seen again in Windsor Great Park last night."[11]

And now to round off, one more encounter from more recent times, which dates from 2012 and told by a member of the Ghost

9 *The Lore of the Land*, programme 3 (Radio 4, 2015).
10 I may be pedantic, but I consider the term "United Kingdom" to be a description, whereas "(Great) Britain" is a proper name.
11 From a newspaper cutting from the *Mercury*, approximately 1970.

Club in their *Ghost Club Journal*. On the 15th November at dusk, he was on his way back from his place of work near the south eastern corner of the Great Park. Suddenly he heard the sound of a hunting horn as well as a yelping pack of hounds, which stopped abruptly. There was no sign of a nearby hunt, and it was the only time this occurred in eight years of using the route for several days per week.[12] Was this Herne?

Although no appearance of Herne accompanied the death of Queen Elizabeth II on 9th September 2022, the bell rang 96 times, marking the number of years of the Queen's long and exalted life.

We have seen Herne and his ghostly hunt appearing in various places with varying kinds of apparitions and noises. He is said to have been seen as far away as Twyford in Berkshire, about 14 miles from Windsor, where a ghostly rider has been recognised by some as Herne. This is quite feasible, since Windsor Forest did once extend that far. So, will Herne appear again? There is no reason to think that he should not reappear, either by himself or with his Wild Hunt. Although there is no doubt that he exhibits some of the racial memory type of ghost, he also appears before national disasters, which are relatively recent manifestations. Perhaps this represents a modern rationalisation of a phenomenon, such as the Wild Hunt, which had lost it relevance to a twenty-first century population. Although to some extent he can be categorised, he refuses to be completely pinned down, and I feel that there is no other ghostly figure like Herne the Hunter.

THE MASK OF HERNE

This chapter concludes with a very strange tale concerning Herne told by the late Michael H.H. Bayley, A.R.I.B.A., Dipl. Arch. Oxford (1922–2013), of Maidenhead in Berkshire, but first some

---

12 https://reallifeghoststories.com/index.php/2018/09/08/herne-the-hunter/

background about this independent and unorthodox history researcher.[13]

Michael Bayley
with antler and piece of the original Herne's Oak
(*Maidenhead Advertiser*)

Architect and historian, Michael Bayley worked for a period in local government, later setting up his own practice working from his home, and he was involved with the Maidenhead Heritage Centre. He was a talented local historian and illustrator, his maps of the local area were highly regarded, and he had a great knowledge of the archaeology, history, folklore and customs of South Buckinghamshire and East Berkshire. However, his interpretation of the origins of local place-names was controversial. His main tenet was that the people living in the areas mentioned above carried on speaking in the "old-fashioned way of speaking" – a Celtic dialect related to Welsh, Cornish and Breton, vestiges of which lasted up until the middle of the nineteenth century. He referred to this as Lowland British, and

---

13 Michael Bayley was a long-standing committee member of the Berkshire Local History Association, and in their newsletter no. 108, of January 2014, was the Chairman's report of his death. He said that he was always delightful to be with, and he recognised his vast knowledge of the east Berkshire area he was brought up in, as well as writing many interesting papers. I myself met him only three or four times, and I can describe him as an old-school perfect gentleman.

when he was young he also recalled his elders using words such as "chinoogle" (meaning hoe), just as in the Cornish language.

His researches led him to believe that many place-names in the area, traditionally derived from Anglo-Saxon or Norman French, could actually be derived from the local Celtic dialect. For instance, he derived the name Windsor from the Celtic WAUN-DA-LES-OR-RES, translating as "the meadow of the bushes of the cattle of the border ford." And for the origin for the town of Maidenhead he came up with MA-E-DDI-EHEDEG, which he translated as "the place of the turbulent stream that goes fast." As you can imagine, such derivations would not be accepted by the English Place-Name Society.

Returning to Herne the Hunter, Bayley had an alternative derivation for his name, viz HER-UN-Y-HUAN TER, meaning "The Challenger of the Bright (Summer) Sun" – denoting the winter Sun God. Allied with this, he mentions a hilltop settlement at Cookham Dean (COC-AM-DIN – "the hill fort village of our ancestors"), which is connected to Windsor Castle, and thence to Herne's Oak, via "Herne the Hunter's Secret Passage." Confirming this alignment, Bayley remarked that the midwinter sunrise as seen from Cookham Dean points to the castle and oak. According to his historical delvings, he found that secret passages radiated from the oak to the prison in the base of the Curfew Tower to Burnham Abbey, about three miles away. But now the strange tale concerning the Mask of Herne, as told by Michael Bayley.

The story concerns a stone head discovered in the garden of the old vicarage situated opposite the Parish Church of St John the Baptist in Windsor High Street. The original building was given to the parish by William Evingdon in 1487, "for the good of his soul" – being the last Keeper of the Great Park, making him a kind of successor to Herne himself. The head was acquired by Michael Bayley's father from the workmen sometime in the early 1930s, when the vicarage was being moved to Park Street, which led to the top of the Long Walk, with the head being named the

"Mask of Herne the Hunter." However, in the mid to late 1930s, the head was claimed and retrieved by the vicar. After World War II, the head was rediscovered in the new vicarage garden. When this property was due to be sold, the head found its way into the Church Museum where it remained until 1963.

Before we continue, a description of the head. The Rev Leslie Badham, Vicar of Windsor, described it as "a curious head with deep-set eyes under the fierce brow and antlered horns,"[14] and as bearing ears which can only be described as those of an animal, not unlike those of a deer. But what is interesting to us are the antlers growing out of the top of his head. The overall effect is that of the Green Man faces which adorn many of our churches and the grotesque figures to be found on the outside of cathedrals placed there to ward off evil spirits. It therefore looked as though it may well have adorned some religious or other building in the past, but Mr Bayley had his own theory as to its origin. He believed that, as it was made in such a way as to allow it to be hung up, it was an emblem of some kind. His conclusion was that it stood for the job of Keeper of the Great Park, which allowed him to be the only person other than the king to hunt deer in the park, since this was confirmed by Shakespeare in *The Merry Wives of Windsor*, where "whoever killed the deer was allowed to wear the hide and horns as a headdress."

The Mask of Herne
drawn by Michael Bayley

14 *The Windsor, Slough and Eton Express*, February 1st 1963, in Petry pp 15–16.

It was at this time that Mr Bayley's views on Herne and his mask appeared in the local press and, a week after publication, the church was broken into and the mask stolen, never to be seen again. Mr Bayley surmised that it was taken by a cult group such as "neo-Satanists," or "some other cranks who thought it was an ancient carving of the Celtic horned god Cernunnos." They could not have been more wrong. One expert decreed that it was an ornament made of coade stone, a hard type of artificial stone used during Victorian times, but Mr Bayley, a qualified architect, did not accept this interpretation and placed it firmly in the fifteenth century.[15]

This would have been the end of Mr Bayley's story except for the fact it has a kind of sequel in the form of a very unusual tale which will not seem relevant until we reach the end. One morning in September, 1856, two boys, William Fenwick and William Butterworth, were standing on a street corner in Windsor when they were offered a lift by a man driving a light horse and carriage. They accepted and were driven to Albany Road, not far from Park Street and the Long Walk, where they became drowsy, and they knew nothing more until they woke up about 5pm, not remembering anything at all. However, they were no longer in Albany Road, but at the end of King Edward VII Avenue at Victoria Bridge over the Thames leading to Datchet.

Upon contacting the police, they gave detailed descriptions of the driver, his horse and his carriage, but no trace could be found of them. Initially the police thought they had been drugged by some unbalanced person, but later they wondered whether the boys had imagined the whole episode, and the case was dropped. But many years later, when he was driving in London, an acquaintance showed William Fenwick a photograph of the Mask of Herne after it had been dug up. Bearing in mind that he was now over 80 years old and the kidnapping incident had taken place when he was about eleven, he had no doubts that the

---

15 From a personal letter from Mr Bayley to this author.

face he then saw was that of the driver who drove him and his friend off to Albany Road all those years ago. So, have we here an appearance of Herne the Hunter in another guise? Who can tell?

Illustration of Herne and his Oak by Michael Bayley

Works Consulted

Kecks, Keddles & Kesh: Celtic Language, Lovespoons and the Cog Almanac, by Michael Bayley (Capall Bann, 1996).
Herne the Hunter: A Berkshire Legend, by Michael John Petry (1972).
The Haunted South, by Joan Forman (Jarrold, 1989).

The Heart of Herne

As this is the final chapter, it is time to unravel the threads that make up the legend of Herne the Hunter. As we have seen, there are several distinct elements contained within the legend, and perhaps it will clarify matters if the key elements are discussed.

First, it can safely be said that if it were not for the phenomenon of deer's yearly growth of a new set of antlers, the legend of Herne would not have taken its present shape. Symbolising, as they do, regeneration and fertility, they impressed early humans so much so that they came to mean something very special to them. As we have seen, people were donning antler headdresses as long ago as 25,000 BP or earlier. Herne in many ways resembles a primitive individual, skilled as he was in the matters of woodcraft and the hunt. Prehistoric communities had a natural affinity with the rest of creation and lived their lives, including the hunting of game, within the context of a kind of ecological spirituality, which industrial humanity has lost.

For the immediate precursor of Herne, however, which in itself owes much to the Palaeolithic hunters; we must look to the Celtic god Cernunnos. Antlered gods were not uncommon in the ancient world, but owing to his popularity on the continent and in Britain, Cernunnos holds a special place in the formation of Herne as a figure. That the horned god was a cult in Britain, its worship continuing through the Roman period, is significant, and it is not impossible that devotion to such a god may well have survived the coming of Christianity. It is entirely likely that, even if worship had ceased, the horned god would have stayed alive in folk memory and folk tales. The arrival of the pagan Saxons may have prompted a revival of such cults, which had not been in the open since the Christianisation of the Roman Empire, and the horned god could have merged with beliefs and mythological characters from the Saxon pantheon. In fact, it has been pointed out that there was a marked degree of similarity between the Celtic and Germanic peoples, especially with regard to religious practices.

For example, Germanic tribes would often sacrifice spoils of war and deposit valuable articles as offerings in lakes or streams – a practice well known in the Celtic world. Classical authors described the two peoples in much the same vein, and both lived adjacent to each other in the heavily forested areas of northern Europe. It is not insignificant that tree worship was important to both cultures. Perhaps we see a local cultural fusion at Windsor, with its sacred mount and oak groves, which kept alive the idea of the horned one, giving rise ultimately to the legend of Herne.

Henry VIII and Herne the Hunter

The Saxons bring us to that strange personage, Woden – the one-eyed, the hooded, the wise, the self-sacrificer, and leader of the Wild Hunt. He has been described as hanging on the World Tree, and the sacrifices made in his honour have their counterparts in Celtic customs. As Wild Huntsman, he is at one with Gwynn ap Nudd from Welsh tradition, which is a remnant of the Celtic culture which covered the whole of Britain before the arrival of the Romans and Saxons. Herne is without a doubt the leader of the Wild Hunt, and his forerunners are to be found in both Celtic and Germanic traditions. Fertility brings us back to the ancient symbolism of antlers and to the power of nature and the abundance of game to hunt. The ideas of sacrifice and renewal were concepts ingrained into the minds of pre-Christian communities, and indeed they were incorporated in the belief systems of the new religion. Thus Herne's death and rebirth into a reinvigorated spirit is a theme which would have taken hold of the imaginations of succeeding waves of peoples who have inhabited our land, bringing the web of connectedness between these threads – all leading us to the figure of Herne.

The magic of numbers is still potent; the number seven being of considerable importance. Odd numbers particularly were thought to have occult significance, and the number three ranked almost as highly as seven. Three was considered to be lucky in both pagan and Christian societies; in the latter case because it denoted the Trinity. Accidents and deaths were expected to occur in threes, which shows that it was ill-luck as well as good luck that was signified. In Celtic times, everything was done in threes, as it featured as their sacred number. Many of their deities had three aspects, and the number linked these gods and goddesses to legends and tales in which Celtic poets enjoyed making use of ingenious play with numbers and letters.

The number three turns up twice in the Herne legend. Firstly, there are the three gifts given to Herne by the king – the silver hunting horn, the golden chain, and the purse of gold coins. Secondly, there are three central characters taking part in the legend – Herne, the king, and Urswick. It can surely be no coincidence that this theme of the number three occurs, which has close links with Celtic beliefs. The veneration of the number is not unknown in Germanic culture. For instance, Woden was one of three brothers, and the Northern goddesses of fate (the Norns) were three in number. Under the names of Urd, Verdandi and Skuld, they were personifications of past, present and future. Apart from weaving the web of fate, their task was to sprinkle daily the tree Yggdrasil with water, and to place fresh clay around its roots. Yggdrasil possessed three main roots – one in Asgard, home of the gods; one in Midgard, the world of men; and one in Niflheim, the underworld. The similarities between the Celtic and Germanic cultures are again emphasised, and provides us with further evidence for the origins of the Herne legend.

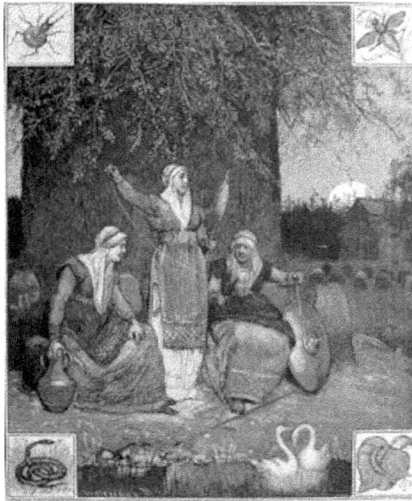

The Norns by L.B. Hansen, 1893
(Wikimedia Commons)

There is a possibility that there was once a custom in Windsor involving a stag mask, although this is obviously mere speculation. But it may help explain the persistence of the legend, and perhaps an antlered figure played a part in a kind of mummers' play many centuries ago. A king, a doctor, a wizard and other strange characters are not unusual figures to find in folk plays, and the theme of the Herne legend is so universal that it is not impossible that this may have once been the case.

What is certain, however, is the folklore which surrounds the oak tree; and its importance in ancient times has been covered earlier. Also is the connection with royalty, such as Charles II, so we should not be surprised to find this. The oak has a long history of being especially important to Berkshire, and we have seen how in fact this significance may have emanated from the Windsor area. What is not in doubt is the fact that a tree was long known as Herne's Oak, and had a considerable tradition to it, just as others throughout Britain. What makes Herne's Oak special, however, is the age of the legend, which Shakespeare confirms dates back to at least the sixteenth century and, as I have shown in this book, probably much further. As to the connections of the oak with stags and antlers – perhaps the origin is in the annual cycle of regeneration. The antlers of the red deer begin to grow anew in May at precisely the time the oak is in flower and, given the similarity of antlers to the branches of a tree, it is likely that the two were considered together as representing the sun's peak of power and intensity.

This association dates back far into prehistory, the depiction of antlers in conjunction with sun symbols being discovered at various sites on the continent; and from Petersfield in Hampshire a Celtic coin found depicting the head of Cernunnos with a sun-wheel set between his antlers was found. The circle and cross are examples of the various ways in which the sun has been represented for many thousands of years. It is apparent that the sun's movement over the seasons, waxing and waning, was linked in the prehistoric mind, with trees losing and growing their leaves again, and stags shedding and re-growing their antlers. Herne's Oak, a midsummer tree, is therefore one aspect of a mythical conception which cannot be separated from the antlers and the dying midwinter sun which form the basis of the seasonal theme of Herne's story.

Cernunnos with sun-wheel between antlers
(Petersfield, Hampshire, destiner.com)

Ghosts, wild hunts and folktales are all examples of humankind's contact with, and an unconscious need of, an otherworldly realm. They put us in touch with another order of reality which all peoples of the world have experienced, some more than others, and which, despite our materialistic world, refuses to go away. Tales of old often strike a chord in our psyche, and recurrent themes occur in many different stories around the globe.

British folklore is especially rich, inheriting elements from as far back, perhaps, as the Neolithic Age, but certainly incorporating aspects from the various cultures of these isles, the Celts, Romans, Saxons, Vikings, and Normans. All have added a particular slant to the melting pot of ideas, beliefs and superstitions which make up the British outlook, be it in the sphere of religion and folklore. The legend of Herne the Hunter is a prime example of the fusion of traditions from many centuries, some specific, and some recurring.

The idea of tree spirits may well be the origin of ghostly appearances in and around forested areas. Ghosts, of course, have featured in history since the beginning of time – and Herne is only one of many strange apparitions which have been encountered and reported. What we have here with Herne, however, is something different. It is not just a matter of classing him as a mere ghost, as I hope the contents of this book have shown. Herne, I feel could only have occurred in Britain, where the specific mix of ancient cultures have provided a background for the appearance of a figure of this type. I think that we have been able to disentangle a number of threads which make up what I feel is the composite figure of Herne. We have woven our way in and out of a number of ideas, and have visited some side-roads en route, and I hope that a better understanding of Herne has been achieved, one that has incorporated all multifarious facets of his nature.

Perhaps Ainsworth did embellish his story somewhat, and invented certain elements, but the themes that he used were certainly relevant, and I am sure that he would not have been unaware of them. Whether Herne the Hunter is seen as a phantom, Wild Huntsman, horned pagan god, shaman, forest spirit or the guardian of Robin the Hooded Man – the durability of his legend is assured.

Loose Ends

And now for some extra matters connected with Herne, which don't fit into the main chapters.

1. There is a possibility that there is an earlier reference to Herne the Hunter than that found in the Shakespeare play. Recorded in a manuscript held in the British Museum dating from around 1520, it reads thus:

> *"Rycharde Horne, yeoman" among names of "hunters whyche be examyned and have confessed" to hunting in His Majesty's forests.*

Also, Herne, Hearn or Hurne are not uncommon surnames, and there is an example dating back to 1279 where a Henry en le Hurne is recorded in the Berkshire hundred rolls, revealing that the name was known in the area. The name comes from "hyrne", which indicated that a person lived on a corner of a plot of land, or on a bend of a river. Whether these persons' names have any bearing on the legend of Herne the Hunter is impossible to tell.

2. The legend of Herne was kept in the popular imagination by a number of printed accounts, which included a Penny Dreadful titled *Herne the Hunter: A Legend of Windsor* from the 1850s.

Penny Dreadfuls were cheap publications which featured stories in weekly parts costing one penny. The stories consisted of such themes as the Gothic, the supernatural, criminals, detectives and vampires; the latter including *Varney the Vampire*, which is one of the earliest tales featuring a vampire in literature. The front covers were illustrated with eye-catching scenes to entice people to want to read the stories therein.

Jack the Devil in an 1838 Penny Dreadful
(Wikimedia Commons)

3. Also in Windsor there was once a Horne Weir on three islands in the River Thames, the name still being used in that of a local field up until the nineteenth century. Whether this has any connection with Herne is not known.

4. Moving further afield, mention must be made of American author, William Perry Brown (1847–1923). He wrote a short story, now very dated, in which he writes about a misogynist character called Herne the Hunter who lives in a cave in a "weird wild region of brake and laurel, walled in by lonely mountains." The story describes him in this way: "Some town-bred Nimrod, with a misty Shakespearean memory, had added to his former patronymic of 'Old Herne' that of Windsor's ghostly visitor. The mountaineers saw the fitness of the title, and 'Herne the Hunter' became widely current." The figure of Nimrod was described in the Bible as "a mighty hunter before the Lord" – thus, once again, we have the link with Herne.

5. Mary Whitehouse (1910–2001) was a conservative campaigner who was against the growing "permissive society", and was the founder and first president of the *National Viewers' and Listeners' Association*. In particular, she had it in for the BBC, which she campaigned against for many years on "blasphemy, crudity and violence" – the latter including *Doctor Who*.

In the 1980s, ITV broadcast a series titled *Robin of Sherwood*, which included the figure of Herne the Hunter – a shamanic spirit of the greenwoods who represented the forces of light and beneficence, and was a guardian of Robin Hood. To Whitehouse, Herne was a pagan figure, strongly in opposition to her Christian faith. The writer of the series, Richard Carpenter, created Herne as a guide for Robin the Hooded Man, who occasionally used magic, for good aims of course. He wrote about Herne as Lord of the Wildwood, based on the pagan idea of the horned god, which modern pagans see as representing nature, they also venerate both a goddess and a god.

Simon Farquar, writing an obituary in *The Independent* after Carpenter's death, made the point that Whitehouse "objected to the [show's] relentless slaughter and blasphemous religious elements, but was deftly silenced by Carpenter in public when he introduced himself to her and the audience by saying 'I'm Richard Carpenter, and I'm a professional writer. And you're a professional ... what?'"[1]

Enough said.

6. Frogmore Cottage is not that far from the site of Herne's Oak, which has had notable people living there. These include Charlotte, Queen Consort of George III, Queen Victoria herself and her mother, the Duchess of Kent, and the Grand Duchess Xenia Alexandrovna, who was exiled due to the Russian Revolution. Recently, the property was briefly leased to the current Duke and Duchess of Sussex, but it had an interesting earlier tenant with an unusual tale to tell.

---

1 *The Independent*, 10th March, 2012, via Wikipedia.

Frogmore Cottage in 1872
(Thomas Ingram, Wikimedia Commons)

This concerns Henry James Senior[2], father of Henry James the novelist, who, in the 1840s, was staying there with his family. In May 1884, after a satisfying family dinner one day, he was sitting alone in front of the fire, in a good state of mind and free from worries. All of a sudden, he was overcome with fear and he trembled all over. He felt that the cause of his terror was an invisible "damned" shape of some sort sitting invisibly in the room, which was emanating evil and vile outpourings affecting life itself. Within about ten seconds, he had been reduced from a sane, contented human being to a nervous wreck. Although diagnosed by doctors as being under stress due to overworking, he was insistent that he was in perfect health both physically and mentally. James then suffered a nervous breakdown, seeing his harrying experience not as spectral or demonic, but a type of cleansing, leading to a spiritual rebirth.

---

2 Henry James Senior was a theologian and father of Henry James the novelist, William James the philosopher, historian and psychologist, and Alice James the diarist. He and his family lived in the cottage in the 1840s.

162

Henry James Senior and Junior, 1854
(Public Domain)

The late author, Colin Wilson, who records the event in his *Mysteries*[3] book, suggested that James may have come into contact with an elemental. If this were the case, Herne is one of many otherworldly spirits which manifest themselves occasionally. Wilson also suggested that the whole of Windsor Great Park was a site of pagan religion connected with the horned god, and with the goddess Diana. It seems clear that certain locations do attract either benign or evil vibrations. With the nearby Herne's Oak and the Fairies' Dell, the area seems to have some kind of elemental and mythical air about it, which unfortunately affected James negatively.

(The only other point on Frogmore Cottage I could find was that when Queen Victoria was there one day, she noticed an "immense numbers of little frogs," describing them as "quite disgusting" – hence the name!)

7. As in no. 6 above, I relate a further instance of the eeriness of the Frogmore/castle area, where Herne, his Oak, and the Fairy

3   See *Mysteries* (1978) by Colin Wilson, pp477–482.

Dell are examples of the manifestations of the mythical and sometimes menacing atmosphere of place.

The late author, Dennis Bardens, related in his book *Ghosts and Hauntings*[4] another ghostly tale involving a Castle Guard. In this case, he was informed by a former Grenadier Guard who told of a young man on guard duty one night at the Long Walk (an eerie posting in itself), which turned out with the soldier shooting himself. A number of weeks later, Bardens' informant, only 18, was posted at the Long Walk. With his two hours nearly up, he heard his relief arriving, so he continued his patrol until his relief came round the corner, upon which he marched back to his sentry box. It was then that he recognised the face of the guard who had shot himself, who presented a smiling, happy face, but then this vision abruptly disappeared, and the relief came round the corner as usual. Back at the barracks discussing the event, it was discovered that the relief had experienced exactly the same thing. It therefore seems that Windsor Castle and its environs are a magnet for strange phenomena.

8. *Herne*, a clothing company based in the UK, describes itself thus:

"Our company takes its name from Herne, the antlered wild huntsman and keeper of the forest. We believe that to be truly at one with nature, just like Herne, outdoor clothing should be natural and sustainable. Founded by Ed Magor in 2016, Herne's vision is to make the finest single source wool outdoor clothing. Products that combine performance and style. Products that have a sense of purpose and a deep connection to the land. Born from a love of the outdoors and field sports, a chance read of Wilderness Hunting & Wildcraft written in the 1920s inspired Ed to investigate the woollen clothes of the pioneers of the American West. At the time, the woollen Stag

---

4 *Ghosts and Hauntings*, by Dennis Bardens (1965), pp202–203.

Shirts were considered the most fundamental piece of outdoor clothing, a must for every adventure and hunt. As we become increasingly aware of the damage we are doing to the natural environment and the harmful effects of synthetic fibres in the ecosystem, a return to woollen outdoor clothing seems nothing short of essential."

9. The *Herne's Egg* (1938) is a play written by W.B. Yeats (1865– 1939), an Irish poet, not long before he died. Described by some as being raucous and abhorrent, including violence, a gang rape, murder and suicide, it also contains humour and is never overly vulgar. A complex verse drama, the play features weird imagery derived from both the Irish and Indian traditions. Yeats was a member of the *Hermetic Order of the Golden Dawn*, and had a lifelong interest in occultism and spiritualism. As to the play's title, it is a bit mysterious. All I can say is that the word "hern" is an archaic version of heron, so it may indicate a heron's egg; perhaps it is symbolic in some way within the play.

William Butler Yeats, 1911
(National Portrait Gallery, Wikimedia Commons)

10. Here I shall quote the opening of *Windsor Castle*, revealing Ainsworth's attraction to the romance of nature:

"In the twentieth year of the reign of the right high and puissant King Henry the Eighth, namely, in 1529, on the 21st of April, and on one of the loveliest evenings that ever fell on the loveliest district in England, a fair youth, having somewhat the appearance of a page, was leaning over the terrace wall on the north side of Windsor Castle, and gazing at the magnificent scene before him. On his right stretched the broad green expanse forming the Home Park, studded with noble trees, chiefly consisting of ancient oaks, of which England had already learnt to be proud, thorns as old or older than the oaks, wide-spreading beeches, tall elms, and hollies. The disposition of these trees was picturesque and beautiful in the extreme. Here, at the end of a sweeping vista, and in the midst of an open space covered with the greenest sward, stood a mighty broad-armed oak, beneath whose ample boughs, though as yet almost destitute of foliage, while the sod beneath them could scarcely boast a head of fern, couched a herd of deer; there lay a thicket of thorns skirting a sand-bank, burrowed by rabbits; on this hand, grew a dense and Druid-like grove, into whose intricacies the slanting sunbeams pierced; on that, extended a long glade, formed by a natural avenue of oaks, across which, at intervals, deer were passing."

Folklore was also an interest of Ainsworth's, and he featured such in *The Lancashire Witches* (1849) about the historic witch trials of Pendle, *Rookwood* (1834) which included the legendary figure of the highwayman Dick Turpin, and *The Flitch of Bacon* (1854). The latter was based around the folk custom of awarding a flitch of bacon to husbands and wives who could swear that they had not regretted their being married for a year and a day. The tradition dates from at least the fourteenth century, and is mentioned by Chaucer. The custom was revived in Victorian days, thanks to Ainsworth's novel, and the Dunmow Flitch is still carried out at Great Dunmow in Essex.

As mentioned earlier, in the case of his novel, *Windsor Castle*, he seems to have used local Windsor folklore, although how much he invented himself is not certain. However, the novel has folkloric themes which were known about in folklore circles.

11. There is a premium bitter beer named *Herne the Hunter*, brewed for the Herne Brewing Company by Wanaka Beerworks in New Zealand. Their recommendation is:

> *"The inaugural brew, this is an Extra Special Bitter, with gentle hop bitterness from the Challenger hops, and deliciously aromatic fruitiness from the Styrian Golding, made from UK malts."*

12. Herne's Oak is a rural locality in eastern Victoria, Australia, which acquired the description of the Haunted Hills because the cattle raised there were easily frightened by the sounds of the night. The name changed to Herne's Oak around 1922, when the play in which the ghost of Herne the Hunter appeared by an oak and scared the cows was performed. Coal mining was carried out, but this ultimately ceased, and the population is now around 500.

13. There is a locality named Herne's Oak situated in Cornwall, south of Launceston. A place of woodland, it is used for leisure activities such as walking, cycling and running. Also nearby is a tree named Herne's Oak, situated in Carmathen Woods, but these appear to have no connection with that at Windsor.

14. An unexpected rendering of the Herne legend surfaced in the 1970s with a series of Western novels by John J. McLaglen. Titled *Herne the Hunter*,[5] they tell of the exploits of a gunslinger named

5   The only notes to add are (1) the author's name, a pseudonym for the writing team of Laurence James and John Harvey; and (2) it is unknown how the series' title came to be called *Herne the Hunter* – was it a coincidence? Anyway, unless you are a fan of Western novels, don't bother!

Jedediah Herne, who was once a bounty hunter known by that name, and who comes out of retirement. Described as a violent man in a violent land whose story takes place in a succession of books advertised as a savage Western series, "Jed Herne was a shootist, a man who lived by the gun: he was Herne the Hunter." He began a trail of vengeance which he embarked upon in the early stories, in which he hunted the seven murderers of his wife and killed them one by one, no matter how long it took or what obstacles crossed his path. Other than the ideas of hunting and dying, the similarity between Jed Herne and the Windsor Herne ends there.

15. *The Rude Man of Dorset* is a song written by folk musician and writer, the late Jerry Bird, editor of *Merry Meet: Journal of Folklore & Pagan Heritage,* about the ithyphallic Cerne Abbas Giant hill figure in Dorset, which is included in *Merry Meet* edition 74, Samhain, 2022. The last verse goes as follows:

> *"Is he Hercules, Helith, the hunter named Herne?*
> *What tribe carved his figure we never will learn.*
> *So proud and erect on this green Dorset hill*
> *He's keeping his secrets. A mystery still."*

Cerne Abbas Giant
(Pete Harlow, Wikimedia Commons)

The song has been recorded by the band, State of Undress – search on Youtube or Spotify. Bird played violin in the band, but he died in early 2023. He published some of my articles in *Merry Meet*, and he is sadly missed.

16. Please note that the place-names of Herne and Herne Bay in Kent, and the town of Herne in Germany, have no connection with Herne the Hunter.

Notable Depictions of Herne in Ainsworth's Windsor Castle

For those who don't wish to read the whole of Ainsworth's novel, here are some passages featuring Herne to relish.

BOOK THE FIRST: ANNE BOLEYN: CHAPTER 1

Suddenly, however, he [the Earl of Surrey][1] was startled by a blue phosphoric light streaming through the bushes on the left, and, looking up, he beheld at the foot of an enormous oak, whose giant roots protruded like twisted snakes from the bank, a wild, spectral-looking object, possessing some slight resemblance to humanity, and habited, so far as it could be determined, in the skins of deer, strangely disposed about its gaunt and tawny-coloured limbs. On its head was seen a sort of helmet, formed of the skull of a stag, from which branched a large pair of antlers; from its left arm hung a heavy and rusty-looking chain, in the links of which burned the phosphoric fire before mentioned; while on its right wrist was perched a large horned owl, with feathers erected, and red, staring eyes.

BOOK THE FIRST: ANNE BOLEYN: CHAPTER 5

The Earl of Surrey … perceived the spectral huntsman and his dogs standing at the edge of the water. The earl instantly

---

1 Henry Howard, Earl of Surrey, was from the nobility and was a poet and politician.

170

shouted to him, and the horseman, turning his head, shook his hand menacingly, while the hounds glazed fiercely at the intruder, and displayed their fangs, but did not bark. As Surrey, however, despite this caution, continued to advance, this huntsman took a strangely-shaped horn that hung by his side, and placing it to his lips, flames and thick smoke presently issued from it, and before the vapour had cleared off, he and his dogs had disappeared.

BOOK THE FIRST: ANNE BOLEYN: CHAPTER 10

After awhile, they arrived at a hillside, at the foot of which lay the lake, whose darkling waters were just distinguishable through an opening in the trees. As the duke was debating with himself whether to go on or retrace his course, the trampling of a horse was heard behind them, and looking in the direction of the sound, they beheld Herne the Hunter, mounted on his swarthy steed, and accompanied only by his two black hounds, galloping furiously down the declivity. Before him flew the owl, whooping as it sailed along the air. The demon-hunter was so close to them, that they could perfectly discern his horrible lineaments, the chain depending from his neck, and his antlered helm. Richmond shouted to him, but the rider continued his headlong course towards the lake, heedless of the call.

The two beholders rushed forward, but by this time the huntsman had gained the edge of the lake. One of his sable hounds plunged into it, and the owl skimmed over its surface. Even in the hasty view which the duke caught of the flying figure, he fancied he perceived that it was attended by a fantastic shadow, whether cast by its ray or arising from some supernatural cause he could not determine. But what followed was equally marvellous and incomprehensible. As the wild huntsman reached the brink of the lake, he placed a horn to his mouth, and blew from it a bright blue flame, which illumined his own dusky and hideous features, and shed a wild and unearthly glimmer over the surrounding objects. While enveloped in this flame, the demon plunged into the lake, and apparently descended to its abysses, for as soon as the duke could muster courage to approach its brink, nothing could be seen of him, his steed, or his hounds.

BOOK THE SECOND: HERNE THE HUNTER: CHAPTER 1

Wyat[2] then stood still, and cried, in a loud, commanding tone – "Spirit, I summon thee! – appear!" At these words, a sound like a peal of thunder rolled overhead, accompanied by screeches of discordant laughter. Other strange and unearthly noises were heard, and amidst the din, a blue, phosphoric light issued from the yawning crevice in the tree, while a tall, gaunt figure, crested with an antlered helm, sprang from it. At the same moment, a swarm of horrible-grotesque, swart objects,

---

2   Sir Thomas Wyat desired Anne Boleyn, as did Henry VIII.

looking like imps, appeared amid the branches of the tree, and grinned and gesticulated at Wyat, whose courage remained unshaken during the fearful ordeal (it is here that Wyat agrees a pact with Herne to regain the attention of Anne Boleyn. Herne agrees with the words *"Your hand upon the compact"* – see illustration below).

BOOK THE SECOND: HERNE THE HUNTER: CHAPTER 5

On the right hand [of the cave], stood a pile of huge stones, disposed somewhat in the form of a Druidical altar, on the top of which, as on a throne, sat the demon-hunter, surrounded by his satellites – one of whom, horned and bearded like a satyr, had clambered the roughened sides of the central pillar, and held a torch over the captive's head.

BOOK THE FOURTH: CARDINAL WOLSEY: CHAPTER II (HERNE THE HUNTER APPEARED TO HENRY ON THE TERRACE)

(At midnight, Henry sees a lightning flash and goes out onto the terrace, where he sees Herne as the storm continues.)

[Abridged]

"You thought you had got rid of me, Harry of England", cried Herne … "What wouldst thou, infernal spirit?" cried Henry. "I am come to keep company with you, Harry," replied the demon … "Avaunt, fiend!" cried Henry, I will hold no converse with thee. Back to thy native hell!" "You have no power over me, Harry," rejoined the demon … for your thoughts are evil, and you are about to do an accused deed. Before … the many great crimes you will commit – I will always appear to you-ha!

Ha! … Harry of England! Your career shall be stained in blood … Better Anne Boleyn had fled this castle … than become your spouse. For you will slay her … Harry of England, thou fierce and bloody king! – Thou shall be drunken with the blood of thy wives; and thy end shall be a fearful one. Thou shalt linger out a living death – a mass of breathing corruption shalt thou become – and when dead, the very hounds with which thou huntedst me shall lick thy blood!" At the close of the latter speech, a flash of lightning of such dazzling brilliancy shot down past him, that he remained for some moments almost blinded; and when he recovered his powers of vision, the demon vanished.

BOOK THE FOURTH: CARDINAL WOLSEY: CHAPTER VII

Certain it was that the sound of diabolical laughter, mingled with the rattling of the chain and sharp blows of the hammer, smote his ears. The laughter became yet louder as Bouchier[3]

3   Sir Humphrey Bouchier, Chancellor of the Exchequer to Henry VIII.

advanced, the hammering ceased, and the clanking of the chain showed that its mysterious wearer was approaching the foot of the steps to meet him. But the captain had not nerve enough for the encounter. Invoking the protection of the saints, he beat a precipitate retreat, and closed the little door at the head of the step after him. The demon was apparently satisfied with the alarm he had occasioned, for the hammering was not renewed at that time.

BOOK THE FIFTH: MABEL LYNDWOOD: CHAPTER IV[4]

The next moment, the demon-huntsman rode from one of the lateral passages into the cave. He was mounted on as wild-looking black horse, with flowing mane and tail, eyes glowing like carbuncles, and in all respects resembling the sable steed he had lost in the forest.

(Herne to Mabel): "Be mine, and you shall accompany me on my midnight rides; shall watch the fleet stag dart over the moonlight glade, or down the lengthened vista. You shall feel all the unutterable excitement of the chase. You shall thread with me the tangled grove; swim the river and the lake; and enjoy a thousand pleasures hitherto unknown to you. Be mine, and I will make you mistress of all my secrets, and compel the band whom I will gather round me to pay you homage. Be mine, and you shall power of life and death over them, as if you were absolute queen. And from me, whom all fear, and all obey, you shall have love and worship."

---

4 Mabel Lyndwood's grandfather was being held at the castle for questioning after an attack on Henry.

BOOK THE SIXTH: JANE SEYMOUR: CHAPTER VIII (THE FINAL SENTENCES OF THE BOOK)

The exclamation was occasioned by a flash of fire from the battlements of the Round Tower, followed by a volume of smoke, and, in another second, the deep boom of a gun was heard. At the very moment that the flash was seen, a wild figure, mounted on a coal-black steed, galloped from out of the wood, and dashed towards Henry [Henry VIII] *whose horse reared and plunged as he passed. "There spoke the death-knell of Anne Boleyn!" cried Herne, regarding Henry sternly, and pointing to the Round Tower. "The bloody deed is done, and thou art free to wed once more. Away to Wolff Hall[5], and bring thy new consort to Windsor Castle!"* (Thus the novel ends with Henry VIII executing Anne Boleyn, enabling him to marry Jane Seymour.)

***

The novel, *Windsor Castle*, is not regarded as "literature", but rather a romance. The author and literary biographer S.M. Ellis, writing in 1911, said:

"[Ainsworth] *adapted and revivified for the purposes of his woodland romance the ancient and weirdly picturesque legend of Herne the Hunter ... [He] continues by claiming that 'Windsor Castle is one of the best examples of Ainsworth's skill in combining a vivid and exciting narrative with a wealth of historical detail and scenic description, the whole interwoven with supernatural events in the most natural manner, so much so that it is difficult to say where the mundane ends and the occult begins. It was an art quite peculiar to this author, who,*

---

5 Wolff Hall is situated on the edge of Savernake Forest, near the village of Burbage. In Tudor times, it was owned by the Seymour family, and Henry VIII visited the manor, where he met Jane Seymour. Ainsworth's novel is basically about Henry's aim to get rid of his then wife Anne Boleyn and marry Jane.

by the force and interest of his narrative, compels the reader to accept his supernatural beings and improbable events as a necessary and essential part of the dramatic work in hand."[6]

The author and academic, Stephen Carver, author of *The Life and Works of the Lancashire Novelist William Harrison Ainsworth, 1805–1882* (2003), commented that the novel's depiction of Herne is "Ainsworth at his gothic best, rivalling Lewis, Maturin and even Byron. Herne effortlessly steals every scene in which he appears, much as he steals souls."[7]

Ainsworth's practice of the mingling of fact and fiction contained in his novels did not appeal to everyone, especially historians, but his books sold well. Fictional elements were thought to be fact in the popular readership, examples being *The Lancashire Witches* (1849) and Dick Turpin in *Rookwood* (1834). Generally, Ainsworth's novels were of their time, not being read much after 1900, especially his antiquated prose style became off-putting. Two of his novels were filmed – *Guy Fawkes* in 1923 (silent), and *Dick Turpin* in 1934.

---

6 https://en.wikipedia.org/wiki/Windsor_Castle_(novel)
7 https://en.wikipedia.org/wiki/Windsor_Castle_(novel)

The Wild Huntsman

BY FELICIA DOROTHEA HEMANS

Portrait of Felicia Dorothea Hemans, *c.*1820
(Wikipedia)

Felicia Dorothea Hemans, nee Browne (1793–1835), was an English poet, who preferred to call herself Welsh by adoption. She could speak six European languages, and two of her well-known poems began "The boy stood on the burning deck" and "The stately homes of England." But here I quote a poem by her on the Wild Hunt:

"Thy rest was deep at the slumberer's hour
    If thou didst not hear the blast
Of the savage horn, from the mountain-tower,
    As the Wild Night-Huntsman pass'd,

And the roar of the stormy chase went by,
　Through the dark unquiet sky!

The stag sprung up from his mossy bed
　When he caught the piercing sounds,
And the oak-boughs crash'd to his antler'd head
　As he flew from the viewless hounds;
And the falcon soar'd from her craggy height,
　Away through the rushing night!

The banner shook on its ancient hold,
　And the pine in its desert-place,
As the cloud and tempest onward roll'd
　With the din of the trampling race;
And the glens were fill'd with the laugh and shout,
　And the bugle, ringing out!

From the chieftain's hand the wine-cup fell,
　At the castle's festive board,
And a sudden pause came o'er the swell
　Of the harp's triumphal chord;
And the Minnesinger's thrilling lay
　In the hall died fast away.

The convent's chanted rite was stay'd,
　And the hermit dropp'd his beads,
And a trembling ran through the forest-shade,
　At the neigh of the phantom steeds,
And the church-bells peal'd to the rocking blast
　As the Wild Night-Huntsman pass'd.

The storm hath swept with the chase away,
　There is stillness in the sky,
But the mother looks on her son to-day,

With a troubled heart and eye,
And the maiden's brow hath a shade of care
Midst the gleam of her golden hair!

The Rhine flows bright, but its waves 'ere long
Must hear a voice of war,
And a clash of spears our hills among,
And a trumpet from afar;
And the brave on a bloody turf must lie,
For the Huntsman hath gone by!"

Felicia began writing poem from an early age, and her first book of poems was published in 1808. In 1812, she married Captain Alfred Hemans, who was an Irish army officer, producing five sons. The marriage failed leaving Felicia to support her family from the proceeds of the sales of her poetry.

Sources

https://allpoetry.com/The-Wild-Huntsman
Wikipedia

Herne elsewhere

Although the origin of Herne the Hunter is firmly in *The Merry Wives of Windsor*, there are two other traditions that have a legend of Herne, plus a possibility. Shakespeare grew up in Stratford-upon-Avon in Warwickshire, surrounded by the woods and forests of the area, and such places are a significant feature of a number of his plays. These accounts cannot be independent legends from the Bard's pen, but they are worth recording.

WORCESTERSHIRE

This tale takes place in the once royal Feckenham Forest, which is about four miles from Redditch. The story starts with the premise that Herne had hunted and killed a white stag, which was a renowned animal in the forest, and was deemed to be sacred to the Abbess of Bordesley Abbey, situated not far from the forest. Having heard the news of the stag's demise, she vehemently cursed Herne who, now under the weight of religious retribution, was doomed to hunt in Feckenham Forest for all time.

Becoming half man and half brute, and with the white stag's antlers emerging from his head, he began his eternal hunts, carrying with him a chain which was reputed to have come from the abbey, where the abbess had planned to mind the stag as a pet.

Tradition has it that Shakespeare, whilst staying for about eight months near Earl's Common in Worcestershire whilst some family trouble was being sorted out, stayed at the Drainer's Arms. It was here that he came up with the idea of Herne the Hunter when he came across an ancient oak there, named the Temple Oak. The tree had associations with the Knights Templar, and it was said the playwright hid in the hollow oak, trying to evade

Jesuit priests looking for those connected with a plot to dethrone Queen Elizabeth I. The story then goes that he transposed the legend of Herne to Windsor. However, there never was an Abbess of Bordesley, but the Temple Oak still stands, estimated to be perhaps well over 1,000 years old.

Works Consulted

Mysteries of Mercia, Hugh Williams, Herne the Hunter & the Temple Oak. https://www.mysteriesofmercia.com (updated: Jan 7th, 2021). *The Folklore of Hereford & Worcester*, by Roy Palmer (1992).

EAST DULWICH

Before being built on, there was once a large expanse of forest named the Great North Wood, which was a natural oak woodland stretching from Croydon to Camberwell. A few remnants remain or were replanted, including Dulwich Wood, Biggin Wood and Beaulieu Heights. In addition, some place-names are evidence of the ancient woodland, such as Norwood, Woodside, Forest

Hill and Honor Oak. Large clearings were well established by the Middle Ages, including the then hamlets of Penge and Dulwich. The earliest record of the wood dates from 1272, and since the Middle Ages coppicing provided timber, oak bark and charcoal.

It is in this area of woodland that author Zoe Hilbert has placed Herne the Hunter in her book *Mischief Acts* (2022), and uses his character, and the Wild Hunt, in a series of sixteen stories which begin in 1392 and finish in 2073. The first deals with the connection of Herne with Richard II, when he was out hunting with his followers, who are jealous of Herne the head hunter, and it continues with what occurred when they decided to act against him. But Herne is injured, being gored by a stag, in the process of defending the king. The Philip Urswick figure, whom Gilbert names as Bearman, removes the stag's antlers and attaches them to Herne's head. He then pours a potion into Herne's mouth, which results in him coming round, but he is not fully restored to his previous strength, and he hangs himself on the Great Oak in the forest. From then on, he becomes a spirit figure and leads the Wild Hunt in its ghostly haunts.

This initial tale is recounted in the form of a prose poem, and here is an extract:

> *"We heard the shouts, in the wood,*
> *And we heard the hoot, the shriek.*
> *He's ours, they called.*
> *We'd missed it. The chance of victory.*
> *The chance to take Herne's place, that was.*
> *For we saw how he was fading.*
> *His fingers all mired in the purple-brown that spilled,*
> *And the king's open mouth.*
> *That was when Bearman came.*
> *Bearman, whose magic sours the wood."*[1]

---

[1] The above is adapted from https://annabookbel.net/mischief-acts-zoe-gilbert-herne-hunter-great-north-wood

The book contains a judicious introduction by Professor Lizbet Gore of Trevone College.

There is a public house on Forest Hill Road in East Dulwich named *The Herne Tavern*, which is a Victorian establishment opposite to Peckham Rye, with a 1930s interior. The local road name, Le Herne Road, is possibly a corruption of Heron Hill, after a haunt of herons, but more probably from a local field named Le Herne, dating from around 1495. In 1883, the road acquired its name, marking the northwest boundary of the previous Manor of Dulwich.

HERNE & BURNHAM BEECHES

As everyone knows, the Wild Hunt is associated with Herne, but I should like to draw readers' attention to another connection with a woodland near where I used to live in Burnham in Buckinghamshire, and that is Burnham Beeches. This vestige of ancient woodland contains the largest collection of old beech trees in the world; renowned for its weird, gnarled beeches, and it is often used as background for films and television. Films include *Goldfinger*, *Robin Hood Prince of Thieves* and *Harry Potter*; and TV productions include *Midsomer Murders*, *New Tricks* and *Doctor Who*. In the past, it attracted people like the poet Thomas Gray and composer Felix Mendelssohn.

The woodland contains an old enclosure officially named Hartley Court Moat, but there are variations. The earliest form is recorded in the foundation charter of nearby Burnham Abbey in 1266, namely 'Hertleigh'. In 1299 it was referred to as 'Herleteye', but by 1596 this had changed to Hartley Wood and Court, and it had been owned by the Eyres of East Burnham. Locally it was known as Hardicanute's Moat, connecting the enclosure with King Canute's son, King Hardicanut, but the dating shows this to be false. Enclosing one and a half acres, it consists of an irregular moat surrounding an area with a continuous bank on the outside and dividing banks within, and the whole is further enclosed by a bank and ditch covering over nine acres.

The date of the site is uncertain, but such moated homesteads are considered to date from the twelfth to the fourteenth centuries, although its origins may well lie in the Anglo-Saxon period or perhaps even earlier. Elsewhere in the woodland there are earthworks dating from the Iron Age Celtic period, so it is obvious that people were here from around at least 300 BCE. One old oak tree in the Beeches is known as Druid's Oak, but obviously it does not date back to the Celtic period, being approximately 800 years old.

Another variation was Harlequin's Moat, a variant of Herian, which was an alternative name for the Saxon god Woden, another leader of the Wild Hunt. First recorded in France in the eleventh century, the legend goes that a monk was chased by a horde of demons known as *familia herlequin*, translated roughly as "herlequin family". This name was the French version of the Germanic Wild Hunt, connected to the English tale of King Herla, whose devilish leader roamed across the countryside accompanied by demons seeking the souls of evil people to take them to Hell. The name changed to Harlequin as the years went by, and Harlequin's Moat could possibly be named after a folk memory of when Woden and his entourage raced through the Beeches, way back in Saxon times. Burnham Beeches is not far north from Windsor, over the River Thames, so can we speculate that it may have been rumoured that Herne himself sometimes led the Hunt through the Beeches?

(An earlier version of this article was first published in the local Burnham Bucks. Newsletter, *Round & About*, issue no. 109, December, 1997/January, 1998.)

Herne the Hunter

OPERAS

Herne the Hunter, or the Days of the Bluff King Hal
A Historical Improbability

The librettist, Thomas Forder Plowman (1844–1919), more known for two of his books, *In the Days of Victoria* and *Fifty Years of a Showman's Life*, penned this comic opera in 1879. It was first performed at the Theatre Royal, Oxford, by the Oxford Amateur Dramatic Society on the 14th and 15th January, in aid of the Oxford Volunteer Fire Brigade. The opera was loosely based on Ainsworth's novel, and the characters included:

Valentine Hagthorne, alias Herne the Hunter (a regular Radical).
Morgan Fenwolf (his First Lieutenant).
Mark Fitton (his Second Lieutenant).
Henry VIII (an absolute Monarch – in his wife's absence), popularly known as Bluff King Hal.[1]
The Earl of Surrey (courtier of the usual stage-type).
Sir Thomas Wyatt (pot, swell, and arch-traitor combined).
Tristram Lyndwood (beadle, town-crier, and "stepparient").
Mabel Lyndwood (the belle of the Royal Borough in the estimation of the young man who *wins her*).
Anne Boleyn (the better half – by a long way – of Henry).
Richard Langdale (the virtuous peasant).
Madge (Valentine's Mamma).

---

1 Bluff King Hal was a nickname of Henry VIII, who invented a game of that name. The players wore blindfolds, and had to kneel down with their heads resting on a block of wood, and they had to guess whom the king was going to wed next!

Others were made up of courtiers, Beef-eaters, beer drinkers, members of Herne's Band, villagers, etc, *ad libitum*.

Engraving of Henry VIII, *c*.1547
(The Rogers Fund, 1922) Public Domain

There were three scenes:

(1) Herne's Oak.
(2) Tristram Lynwood's Cottage.
(3) The Cavern beneath Herne's Oak.

The Date of Action: Pinnock's Catechism.[2]
The Locality: Windsor.
Costumes: Harrison Ainsworth's *Windsor Castle*, as illustrated by Cruikshank.

---

2 William Pinnock (1782–1843) started adult life as a schoolmaster, and later as a book seller, publishing inexpensive educational works. The first publications were a series of Catechisms, basically short popular works formed as questions and answers on a range of topics, intended "for the instruction of children." I have not been able to find out what the Catechisms have to do with a date.

Here I shall try to convey the gist of the opera:

The Prologue

(This is quite lengthy, so I have selected what is most relevant to Herne.)

"The literature which never failed our young minds to entrance
Was a high-spiced form of novel-the historical romance;
And first and primest favourite, who furnished forth such fare,
Was Ainsworth; his weird mysteries were grand beyond compare.
A circulating library – a well-spring of delight –
Supplied us with material to spoil rest at night,
And caused us oft to start up in an agony of dread,
As Imagination pictured spectral headsmen round our bed.
At night, instead of letting our young minds in sleep lie fallow,
Illumined by the dim light of the surreptitious 'tallow',
We gloated o'er its pages, and our youthful bosoms thrilled
At the deeds of Herne the Hunter, which our very marrow chilled.
And as we heard the iron tongue proclaim from belfry tower,
In solemn tones, the awful fact – the witching midnight hour,
We feared as every minute drop of blood ran colder,
That the grim and ghostly huntsman was pr'aps peeping o'er our
shoulder.

So when I'm asked to find a play, and look out for a theme,
I'm haunted by the shadowy forms, suggestive of a dream,
Of the demon of the forest and his ghastly crew, who stand
As Cruikshank has depicted 'em, a fearful-looking band.

The ghostly attributes of Herne I've been obliged to drop;
Folks don't believe in spirits now unless they go to shop
And buy 'em, and of late I've heard it very often stated
K'en then they don't believe in 'em – they're so adulterated.

And so I've renovated Herne and modernized his crimes
To suit the present altered circumstances of the times.
I only hope you'll think my piece, at any rate, the pains worth,
And if you do I'm much obliged to you and Mr. Ainsworth."

The Opera

The humorous, and romantic, tale is quite different from Ainsworth's novel, *Windsor Castle*, and is very comical throughout. Plowman has made Herne into a human being rather than a spirit, becoming Valentine Hagthorne, a freedom fighter together with his band of men. Herne's Oak seems to be some kind of portal, since people go in and out of its trunk and down into a cavern beneath throughout the opera. I shall concentrate on the character of Herne (Valentine).

Valentine Hagthorne's band, having killed a rabbit for eating, sing the following:

"But higher game we'll fly at – Revolution!
Death to all rabbits and the Constitution.
A day will come, ha! ha! we're close upon it,
When every British bobby, we will bonnet,
No longer slaves, we'll all be free – Hooray!"

"Look out for Emancipation Day." (sung by Valentine)

Moving on, Valentine sings:

"We're the radicallist radicals that ever you did see,
Nor e'en in Clerkenwell you'll find such levellers as we.
We poach the king's preserves and prig a purse when e'er we can,
For wealth should be distributed, so says the 'Rights of Man.'"

As you can see, Valentine is part freedom fighter, and part Robin Hood.

Next, upon Tristram worried about encountering Herne, Valentine says:

> *"Your fears allay, He disappears, they say, at break of day.*
> *Besides, you know, he's such an awful fright,*
> *(solemnly) He wears great horns and looks as black as night.*
> *He's leagued, too, with Old Nick, so I've been told –"*

> *"Here, don't – you make my very blood run cold."* (said by Tristram)

Much later, Valentine reappears and adds these words:

> *"To liberty we'll quickly march away,*
> *Near at hand's Emancipation Day.*
> *My soul's in arms and eager for the fray.*
> *Hurrah for Herne the Hunter and his band."*

Now Valentine, having been trying to court Mabel but had been scorned, says to her:

> *"Yes, you who scorned, refused me, and made fun o' me,*
> *Swore when I pressed my suit that you'd have nine o' me.*
> *It's my turn now –"*

Mabel replies:

> *"What mean you? Speak! Explain!"*

Valentine retorts:

> *"Look out! Hey, presto!* (suddenly throws off disguise, antlered helmet, moustache, etc, and appears in his 2nd dress)

Here we are again! (à la Clown)
You called me once a country clown, I ween.
Oh, be my bride, give me your heart and hand,
And you shall be the queen of Herne's famed band."

However, Mabel loves another. The other theme of the opera is that of wooing by King Henry of Anne Boleyn, which comes to fruition. The final words of the opera are:

"A halo, then, of happiness pray fling (King Henry)
O'er Herne the Hunter – (Valentine/Herne)
Aye, and Hal the King." (King Henry)

The opera ends with the chorus singing *"Let the Air"* from Gilbert and Sullivan's *H.M.S. Pinafore*.

I hope that this condensation renders some of the flavour of this comic opera, especially of Herne the Hunter.

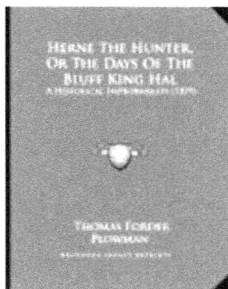

HERNE THE HUNTER: A LEGEND OF ROYAL WINDSOR. AN OPERA IN THREE ACTS

On Wednesday14th December, 1887, a performance of the above took place in the New Town Hall in Reading, Berkshire. The opera's libretto was written by Edward Oxenford (1846–1929), a playwright, poet and critic; and the music composed by John Old

(1827–1892). The following is an abridgement of the review of the opera in *The Berkshire Chronicle* of Saturday, December 17th, 1887.

The opera begins with Herne appearing in the ballroom at the castle, and carries away Constance, the bride of Lord L'Estrange. Constance is rescued from the demon hunter and married her lover, which ended the opera. The reviewer stated that operas fall into four categories: historic, domestic, comic and mythical – judging that this one is a combination of the historic and the mythical, making the work more interesting.

Apparently, the opera "abounds with dramatic situations, of which the music is admirably descriptive. The weird-like character of some of the principal actors in it requires a musical setting of an exceptional nature, but the composer is always equal to the occasion. With a first class band and a well drilled chorus, the composer gave an excellent representation of the work." The cast was as follows:

Herne (baritone), played by Mr Otto Fischer.
Lady Constance (the King's ward, soprano), played by Miss Agnes Larkcom.
Anne Boleyne (the Queen, mezzo-soprano), played by Miss Edith Barnard.
Lord L'Estrange (betrothed to Lady Constance, tenor), played by Mr Henry Guy.
The Captain of the Guard (tenor), played by Mr Henry Guy.
A Hunter (Herne's followers, bass), played by Mr Huggins.
King Henry VIII (bass), played by Mr Henry Pope.

There follows a lengthy rundown of the story, which is too much to repeat in detail here, so I present the "core" of the story, but without the songs and music.

Herne makes his first appearance at a ball held in Windsor Castle, where suddenly Herne's horn is heard, startling the guests. Then his voice calls out outside, saying: "The Lord of the Forest am I," with his band joining him in a mocking chorus. Next, L'Estrange recites the legend of the demon hunter. This is followed by the sound of Herne's horn again, accompanied by demonical laughter, as well as the sound of a hideous rabble. The orchestra plays snatches of Herne's song, and the hunter suddenly appears. Despite the King ordering Herne's capture, he is met by mockery and defiance, and he carries off Constance amid the exultant laughter of his followers.

He takes Constance to a ruined chapel where a painting of a nun is hanging, which Herne sees as a resemblance to his victim, leaving her alone. Later, he returns asking for forgiveness, but Constance scorns him, leading to threats against her. Next, his band rush in, but become surrounded by the Royal Guards, who quickly rescue Constance, at which Herne vanishes, singing his defiant song. Back at the castle, Constance becomes insensible and L'Estrange tries to wake her back to life and joy, and he manages to assure her that she is safe. The King proceeds to sanction the marriage between the two, but as the ceremony takes place in a nearby chapel, Herne and his band are heard, but they are powerless. The scene changes to the castle, where the royal procession enters, and "the whole is admirably worked up, and forms a fitting conclusion."

The air announcing the appearance of Herne was admirably sung by Mr Henry Guy, who was in good voice throughout. Mr Otto Fischer sang the rollicking song of Herne, "The Lord of the Forest am I," with spirit and power, though at times he was out of tune. The opera contained no spoken dialogue, but Old's music was competent and often tuneful, with occasional adventurous, but also amateurish, harmonic excursions. Though there were a few slight slips, the choruses

were generally well attacked. There were no encores, but while
thanking the audience for their approval, the magic was too
exacting on a first night's performance, and the work was too
heavily scored to admit them.

The reviewer was obviously much taken with the performance, which featured a first class band and a well drilled chorus. It abounded with dramatic situations, of which the music was admirably descriptive. I am sure that it must have been a very enjoyable evening, and there was loud applause.

The song relating the story of the legend of Herne the Hunter, sung by Mr Otto Fischer, is retold here:

> *"'Tis nigh two hundred years ago,*
> *That Herne was Hunter to the Crown,*
> *And none so deft with spear and bow,*
> *As he who still enjoys renown.*
>
> *He'd bring to earth the fleetest hind,*
> *Defy the fiercest boar at bay,*
> *Train up the hawk, the bugle sound,*
> *Unearth the fox, the badger slay.*
>
> *But soon a gentler task arose,*
> *He sought to win a maiden's heart;*
> *Of love he felt the keenest throes,*
> *And bared his breast to Cupid's dart.*
>
> *The maid he loved was vowed to God,*
> *A nun within a convent nigh;*
> *Yet from the holy paths she trod,*
> *He wean'd her feet, alas! To die!*

For soon, in fit of jealous rage,
He slew the maid he loved so well;
And in remorse, the sinner's wage,
A self-made gift to death he fell.

Chorus: *Yes, on that withered oak he died,*
A murderer and a suicide.

And since the day he joined the dead,
He roams at night the forest land,
With antlers on his ghostly head,
Surrounded by a phantom band ...

Chorus: *O! Monstrous fiend, from depths infernal,*
May thy tortures be eternal."

HERNE LE CHASSEUR

This opera, now lost, was an adaptation of *The Merry Wives of Windsor*, in which Herne the Hunter played the title role. The work was by the French musician, Francosi-Andre Danican Phildor (1726–1795), and dates from 1773. He was born into a musical family, and he composed twenty comic operas, as well as secular motets and cantatas. He also wrote the music for the rituals required by the Freemasons, being a member of Les Neuf Soers (The Nine Sisters) Lodge, which had a musicians offshoot society named the Societe Apollonienne (Apollonian Society). In addition, he was a first class chess player.

DIE LUSTIGEN WEIBER VON WINDSOR

Composed in 1845/46 by the German, Carl Otto Nicolai (1810-1849), the opera *The Merry Wives of Windsor* featured Falstaff disguised as Herne the Hunter. He was born in Konigsberg in Prussia and was a musical child prodigy. He was one of the founders of the Vienna Philharmonic Orchestra, and he composed four other operas. He died of a stroke only a couple months after the premiere of the opera, which is still popular in Germany.

Originally, Nicolai found it difficult to find anywhere that would present the opera, but eventually it was performed at the Konigliches Opernhaus (Royal Opera House, now the Berlin State Opera) in 1849, with the composer conducting, but it was not a success, being cancelled after only four performances. It was only sometime after Nicolai's death that it started to become popular. The music itself is considered to be of high quality, and it has been performed more and more over the years, up until the twenty-first century. Nicolai also composed an overture of the work which has been recorded.

In the 1940 film, *Falstaff in Vienna*, Nicolai was played by Hans Niselsen.

FALSTAFF

This opera was composed by Verdi (1830–1901), with the libretto by Arrigo Boito (1842–1918), which was improvised on materials from the Shakespeare plays *The Merry Wives of Windsor* and parts from *Henry IV*. Both were Shakespeare addicts, but Verdi decided to veer from his usual subject matters of a heroic nature so that he could "have at last the right to laugh a little." The comic opera, as in the Shakespeare play, details the attempts of Sir John Falstaff to seduce two married women in order to get hold of the wealth of their husbands. In the last moonlit act (set in Windsor Great Park), Falstaff, characters disguised as spirits, and the ghostly "Black Huntsman" or Herne the Hunter appear.

FALSTAFF OSSIA LE TREBURLE (FALSTAFF, OR THE THREE TRICKS)

Antonio Salieri (1750–1825) composed an opera titled as above in 1799, the libretto was written by Carlo Prospero Defranceschi, who condensed the plot into two acts, dropping some of the characters. The opera specifically makes mention of Herne.

MERRIE ENGLAND

This comic opera was written by Basil Hood, his libretto set to music by Sir Edward German, and was first played at the Savoy Theatre in London in 1902–1903. It is set in Windsor, and includes mention of folklore, mythology and witchcraft, featuring English characters such as Robin Hood, St George and the Dragon, Sir Walter Raleigh, Queen Elizabeth and, of interest to us, the Earl of Essex and Long Tom, a Royal Forester. Essex arranges for Long Tom to impersonate Herne the Hunter and to be seen by the Queen as an apparition, choosing Essex for herself. In this version, Herne appears only when a king or queen considers committing a crime. The opera is set in the court of Queen Elizabeth, who is visiting Windsor to celebrate May Day, with love and various rivalries taking place surrounding the Queen.

German's music for the opera has been seen as one of the most tuneful and uplifting English works of its kind.

Merrie England was recorded first by HMV in 1918, on a set of ten 78rpm discs; and again in 1960, on a set of 33rpm discs. A few complete recordings have been issued, and a number of songs from the opera have been recorded on many occasions. Of note, the work was performed at Queen Elizabeth's jubilees for her Silver (1977), Golden (2002), and Diamond (2012).

SIR JOHN IN LOVE

Adapted from the play by Ralph Vaughan Williams, it features an impersonation of Herne in order to misguide Falstaff.

VICTORIA AND MERRIE ENGLAND

The Legend of Herne the Hunter was part of an 1897 ballet by Arthur Sullivan, depicting scenes from British history and folklore.

HERNE THE HUNTER

Meyer Lutz (1829–1903), British but German-born, composed the cantata for the above named opera, first performed in 1862, at the Crystal Palace in London. Below is the frontispiece for the score of *A Valse on Favourite* [sic] *Airs from W.M. Lutz's Dramatic Legend*, by Charles Coote.

Herne in the Media

The items I have included below are a selection that I have chosen myself. Generally, I have not included those of an obscure or minor interest, but these can be found online.

MUSIC

Herne the Hunter

1. The 1984 album by Clannad titled *Legend* was the soundtrack for the ITV series *Robin of Sherwood*. Herne the Hunter is the Spirit of the Forest in the series, and is represented by the track titled simply *Herne*, a very atmospheric piece, as is the whole album (see also below and chapter *Loose Ends*).

2. S.J. Tucker performs a song titled *Hymn to Herne* from her 2007 album, *Blessings*.

3. A release by Hadley Fraser includes the song *Herne and the Red Kite* on his 2014 EP titled *Just Let Go*.

4. A song titled *Longing for the Woods Part III: Herne's Prophecy* was a track on the 2004 album *Far from the Madding Crowd* by the Danish band Wuthering Heights.

5. *Face of the Hunter*, music by the pagan metal band Herne (2011 album).

6. A 12-minute instrumental track *Herne the Hunter* by the rock band Marillion can be found on their album *Early Demos and Sessions 1979–1981* (now a collector's item). However, one can listen to it on Youtube.

The Wild Hunt

1. In 1939, there was a popular American cowboy song, *Riders in the* Sky, in which the homeless dead are a ghostly "devil's bed" of cattle whose "brands wuz still on fire" and whose "hooves wuz made of steel" – while Woden is represented as a ghostly cowboy condemned to a terrible eternity of rounding-up "across these endless skies." The song was first recorded in 1948 by Stan Jones, with versions by such artists as Burl Ives, Bing Crosby, and Peggy Lee (all in 1949), and the Ramrods (1961) who had a USA no. 30 chart hit with an instrumental take, reaching no. 8 in Britain. This last version had overdubs of eerie cattle calls, shouts and whistles. The most well-known version in more modern times was that by The Blues Brothers in the film, *Blues Brothers 2000*.

Allied to the above is the track recorded by the rock band, The Doors, titled *Riders on the Storm*. Written by the late vocalist Jim Morrison, it was released as a single in June 1971, which hit the USA charts the same week that Morrison died. It was known to have been influenced by the song discussed above, and it was inducted into the Grammy Hall of Fame in 2010.

2. The Tallest Man on Earth, a Swedish singer-song writer, recorded an album titled *The Wild Hunt* in 2010.

3. The Swedish black metal band Watain also released an album titled *The Wild Hunt* in 2013.

4. Classical interpretations of the Wild Hunt include:

(i) *Wilde Jagd* (Wild Hunt), by Franz Liszt.
(ii) *Le Chasseur Maudit* (The Accursed Huntsman), by Cesar Franck – based on Gottfried August Buger's ballad, *Der Wilde Jager* (The Wild Hunt).

BOOKS

1. There have been quite a few Herne appearances in books. However, there is one I should like to bring to the reader's attention, and that is the book entitled *The Dark is Rising* by Susan Cooper, published in 1973 – the second of a series of five linked children's novels featuring British folklore and legends, which adults can appreciate as well. *The Dark is Rising* is set in south Buckinghamshire, where Cooper was brought up. It tells the story of Will, an eleven-year-old boy living with his family in the village of Huntercombe, who is last of the Old Ones, who had to find and join together the five remaining Signs of the Light to prevent the Dark from rising. Being set in the Thames Valley, it is not surprising that Herne the Hunter makes an appearance, as does Herne's Oak.

The book interweaves ancient Celtic and English traditions with local legends and folklore tales of Buckinghamshire, which add to the atmosphere of the tale. As one reviewer put it: "It is almost as if the magic forces within the story were themselves reaching out to spellbind the reader." Cooper also brings in Herne in the last of the series, *Silver on the Tree*, and this author cannot recommend the series too highly – and I mean books, for there is also a film (see below).

The full sequence is as follows:

Over Sea, Under Stone (1965).
The Dark is Rising (1973) – features Herne.
Greenwitch (1974).
The Grey King (1975).
Silver on the Tree (1977) – features Herne.

The Seeker: The Dark is Rising is an American film released in 2007, based on the book. An American family, including Will, move to a small English village from whence Will's ancestors originated. In fact, the film was made in Romania, which about sums up the scenario. The legend and folklore of the book has all been deleted and, worst of all, Herne the Hunter does not even make an appearance! The film was obviously influenced by those of Harry Potter – and Susan Cooper herself was not impressed by the result, to say the least. In my estimation, I would rate it at 3 stars out of 10. If you like fantasy, have any interest in British legends and folklore and enjoy a real, engaging read, then get hold of the books – you will not regret it!

2. *Wondrous Strange* is the debut novel by Lesley Livingstone, published in 2008. In the story, Herne is a hunter from the olden days, and a lover of Queen Mabh (who appears in Shakespeare's play *Romeo and Juliet* as the Queen of the Fairies). She gives Herne an enchanted horse, and along with the main character, a teenage actress, the story unfolds.

3. A series of comic books titled *Hellboy: The Wild Hunt* written by Mike Miglona, which features Arthurian and Irish legend, includes a band of British noblemen who have named themselves The Wild Hunt, with a character who plays Herne the Hunter.

4. The aptly named fantasy author, Kevin Hearne, features Herne in the sixth volume of the *Iron Druid Chronicles*, titled *Hunted*, published in 2013.

5. A series of books titled *Wild Cards*, published from 1987–2022, is a science fiction/super hero work, written by over 40 authors, and the setting is an alternate post-World War II USA. The character Dylan Hardesty is a mutant who transforms into Herne the Huntsman during the night-time hours. He is eight feet tall and can make anyone become full of bloodthirsty rage when they hear Herne's horn, and in doing so the Gabriel Hounds are also summoned.

6. Jane Yolen's book titled *The Wild Hunt,* published in 1995, features two boys living in parallel times, a talking cat, The Hunt, and Lord Herne – which is the true name of the Horned King (also referred to as the Horned Man, the Hunter of Dark, and the Master of Winter). He represents "… the dark, the night, the cold. He is chaos and anger and war."

7. In Terry Pratchett's *Discworld* series, a character named Herne the Hunted is featured. He is portrayed as a deity of small animals that inhabit woodlands; but unfortunately, he is also hunted himself, leading him to acquire a sly nature in order to avoid being put to death, which results in him being able to run very fast. As to his appearance, his height is three feet, and he has ears like a rabbit, as well as two small horns.

8. *Herne the Hunter* is the title of a collection of poems by Peter McDonald, one of Ireland's most accomplished poets. He deals with myth and storytelling via Herne's legend, with subjects from game animals to constellations, his Herne being not quite man, spirit nor beast.

9. Herne appears in *The Bitterbynde Trilogy* by Cecilia Dart-Thornton as a powerful "unseelie wight". As Lord Huon, he hunts for the chief protagonist along with his hell hounds.

10. Herne makes appearances in *Marvel* and *DC* comics.

11. Herne appears in C.E. Murphy's 2005 *Urban Shaman* sequence.

12. Herne or, as he is also referred to, Cernunnos, is a character in *The Alchemyst: The Immortal Secrets of Nicholas Flammel* (2007), a fantasy by Michael Scott.

13. In the fantasy novel *Cold Days* (2013) by Jim Butcher, the Erlking is known as Lord Herne.

14. *A Book of Herne* (1981) by Eric Mottram is a volume of poetry on the myth of Herne (now scarce).

15. *Daughter of the Morning* (2009) by Kara Hughes is a novel featuring Herne, Galahad, Cernunnos, Marian and Robin, Ambrosius, Morgana, Merlin and Niniane. A girl on her first visit to Windsor begins to see the spirits of the trees and lake. She is the last of the Ancient Ones and Guardian of the Light. According to prophecies made over 100 years prior, she and Herne battle the Dark forces, when she would become Herne's saviour.

16. *Herne the Hunter: A Berkshire Legend* by Michael John Petry (1972) mainly deals with the Wild Hunt.

17. *In Search of Herne the Hunter* by Eric L. Fitch (1994).

Note

In the books and music references, some could have since been transferred into audio books, computer games, DVDs and other electronic media. Since I am not that au fait with digital matters, I shall leave the matter here, but please see the section below for those I have been able to identify.

ELECTRONIC MEDIA

1. The *Robin of Sherwood* TV series (1984–1986) includes Herne the Hunter (see *Books* above, and the chapter *Loose Ends*). It shows a shamanic side to Herne, who influenced Robin to adopt the title of the "Hooded Man".

Herne represents the powers of light and darkness, teaching and assisting Robin the Hooded Man and his band. Robin received his magical sword named *Albion* and his longbow from Herne. The series has been issued on VHS, DVD and Blu-Ray, and the author, Richard Carpenter, also novelised the stories.

2. The author, John Masefield, wrote the children's fantasy novel *The Box of Delights* in 1935, a sequel to the earlier novel *The Midnight Folk*. Recent reissues of the book are available now. In 1984, it became a TV series, with Patrick Troughton (the second Doctor Who), and it has been issued on VHS and DVD. Herne appears in the story, and the soundtrack was issued on CD in 2018, which includes a track titled *Herne the Hunter*.

3. *Call of the Hunter* (2009) is a film built around Herne the Hunter. It concerns a crew making a documentary film on Herne at a manor house somewhere in Britain, but one by one they die horribly in gory ways, with the survivors trying to discover what Herne wants from them. Viewer ratings show this film to be very low, and I must agree (although one scene has an actor holding a copy of my 1994 *In Search of Herne the Hunter* book!).

4. A *Doctor Who* CD audio adventure titled *Leviathan*, a story never filmed from the Colin Baker years, includes an appearance by Herne the Hunter.

5. In series 2 #56 of *Monster In My Pocket*, amongst a throng of fantasy monsters, Herne the Hunter is included. It can be found on a video game, trading cards, books, toys and comic books.

6. A digital collectable card game *Magic: The Gathering* features a Master of the Hunt and Master of the Wild Hunt, based on Herne.

7. An NPC character in the game *World of Warcraft: Shadowlands Expansion* named Lord Herne is a kind of male dryad, and part of the Wild Hunt faction in the multiplayer online role-playing game.

8. In issue 26 of the *Green Arrow* comic book series, Herne is a forest spirit resembling a tree, also in the 2004 *The Bard's Tale* adventure video game.

9. The video game titled *Assassin's Creed Valhlla* has Herne as a cryptic and powerful figure. In that role, he is venerated by Viking warriors.

Herne the Hunter

Yuletide is a magical and mysterious time in which to celebrate the survival of Berkshire's most enduring legend – Herne the Hunter. Join us in an evening devoted to exploring this mythic archetype and the ancient importance of Midwinter with two local experts and a lively crowd who intend to celebrate this holiday event with merriment and good company.

FEATURING

James Bennett

Tutor in Archaeology for Continuing Education, Reading University

And ...

Eric L. Fitch

Local Historian and author of *In Search of Herne the Hunter*, and *Unknown Taplow*

FRIENDS MEETING HOUSE (QUAKERS), 74 RAGSTONE RD, SLOUGH

WEDNESDAY 17th December, 8pm

PRESENTEND BY SLOUGH4PEACE

www.slough4peace.net

(A poster for a talk by myself some time ago)

TIME-LINE

BCE

c20000 Palaeolithic cave paintings (The Sorceror).

c8500 Mesolithic Age commences (Star Carr antler headdresses).

c5000 Neolithic Age commences (ritual antler deposits).

c2300 Bronze Age commences (reverence of the oak first recognised).

c800 BCE–43 CE Celtic Iron Age (worship of Cernunnos).

CE

43 Roman invasion of Britain under the Emperor Claudius.

410 Romans depart from Britain.

c450 First Anglo-Saxons in Britain (worship of Woden).

c700 Theodore, Archbishop of Canterbury, condemns those who dress in animal skins.

793 First Vikings in Britain (worship of Odin).

1127 Sighting of the Wild Hunt at Peterborough.

1154 Sighting of King Herla and his Wild Hunt.

1283 Sighting of the Wild Hunt near York.

1377 Richard II ascended the throne (and later encountered Herne).

1400 Death of Richard II (and recommencing of Herne's hauntings).

1413 The shouts of the Wild Huntsmen heard on the eve of Henry IV's murder.

c1450 The Mask of Herne is created.

1597 *The Merry Wives of Windsor* is first performed.

1783 Herne's Oak bears acorns for the last time.

1789 Herne's Oak bears leaves for the last time.

1796 Herne's Oak felled in error.

1838 Another oak erroneously suggested to be Herne's Oak.

1843 W. Harrison Ainsworth's novel *Windsor Castle* published.

1863   Erroneous Herne's Oak blown down and replaced by Queen Victoria.

1906   Victoria's replacement tree cut down.

1906   Herne's Oak II planted by Edward VII where the original oak was felled in 1796.

c1933   Discovery of the Mask of Herne.

1963   Disappearance of the Mask of Herne.

1972   Publication of the first book on Herne, *Herne the Hunter: A Berkshire Legend* by Michael John Petry.

1994   Publication of *In Search of Herne the Hunter*.

2024   Publication of this volume.

As is more customary nowadays, I use BCE (Before the Common Era – BC) and CE (The Common Era – AD), as well as BP (denoting Before the Present).

A wicker sculpture of the Horned God by Ethan Doyle White
Museum of Witchcraft and Magic, Boscastle, Cornwall
(Wikimedia Commons)

The Strange Tale of Herne the Hunter of Windsor Forest

A STORY FOR YOUNGSTERS

Many centuries ago, in magical times so different from our own, when fairies, witches and dragons were believed in, there lived a forest keeper by the name of Herne who was employed on the royal estate at Windsor Forest. Skilled in woodcraft and hunting, he worked as a loyal subject in the service of the King. Whenever the court was in residence at Windsor Castle, the King would enjoy nothing more than the thrill of the chase. Herne, with his expert knowledge of woodland wildlife, would guide the King to the most favourable hunting spots. On such occasions, he was always accompanied by his two hounds, both black and swift of foot.

Thus it was that one day a royal hunt left the castle gates in search of game. The King was joined by his noblemen and foresters, including Herne, together with their hordes, hounds, bows and arrows. They had already covered some miles when a fine stag with a splendid head of antlers was spotted by the party. In no time at all, the chase was on and the hunters began to gain on the stag, but could only manage to wound the animal. However, the King and Herne soon broke away from the others and gradually caught up with the beast, which was now in some pain.

Adult male red deer (Pearson Scott Foresman, Public Domain).

As they neared the animal, it suddenly stopped and turned. The startled King's horse threw its rider to the ground, whereupon the stag, with its head down and its antlers forward, made straight for the King. With the speed of lightning, Herne jumped down from his steed. He then hurled himself between the King and this Lord of the Forest and caught the full impact of the charging animal. The King sat up and, as he stood up and steadied himself, managed to witness Herne plunging his knife into the stag's throat.

Overcome with gratitude, the King rushed over to Herne, only to find his devoted servant lying almost under the stag, fatally injured. He lay there immobile with blood gushing from his side, whilst the King ran excitedly backwards and forwards in despair. It was then that the rest of the hunting party arrived on the scene.

"Help!" Exclaimed the King. "Herne has saved me from certain death, but he himself lies here at death's door. Who can save him?" The foresters gathered around and found Herne blooded and barely breathing. It did not take them long to realise that death was not far off and they turned, long-faced, to the King.

Aghast, he raised his face and arms skywards and cried, "By heaven, this cannot be! What can be done to save this loyal and selfless subject?" There was silence amongst all the party, each one averting his gaze from the King. They began to make their way back to their horses, whilst the grieving monarch looked around in anguish.

At that moment, as if from nowhere, a rider appeared mounted on a jet-black horse. All eyes turned on him. As the stranger dismounted, the King could see that he was dressed in brown, with loose-fitting tunic and breeches. Round his shoulders he wore a dark green cloak and upon his nearly bald head was a skull-cap partially surrounded by a fringe of white hair.

Taking his staff and a leather bag from his horse, he stepped towards the King announcing, "Sire, I can affect a cure for your ailing servant. My magical powers can make him well once again, should you so desire." The King readily agreed and made a promise that, upon his return to health, Herne would be promoted to the post of Head Forester. The King was so anxious about losing his best forester that he asked, "Please make haste, for he may soon die."

At which the wizard, which we must to call him, approached the prostrate figure of Herne. As he did so, he made strange movements with his staff and mumbled incantations under his breath. He then knelt down, placed his bag and staff onto the ground and gently moved Herne from the stag.

Untying his bag, he produced from it three objects. The first was a wooden container from which he proceeded to sprinkle a fine dust in the shape of a circle around himself, Herne and the stag. The second was a woodman's knife and, to the King's amazement, he used this to cut off the antlers from the stag's head, carefully keeping intact the top of the skull to which they were attached. However, the King was even more astonished when the wizard lifted the antlers and placed them upon Herne's head, tying them on with the third item from his bag – a set of leather thongs.

The wizard then directed the foresters to gather twigs and stout oak branches so that a stretcher could be constructed. This done, they placed Herne's body, complete with antlers, onto it. "Farewell," said the wizard, "Herne shall return healed within one month," to which the King agreed. Having spoken, he walked over to his horse, whispered something to it and mounted. Leading the way, with the foresters following with Herne on the stretcher, he proceeded to his secret hut in Windsor Forest.

However, as the band made its way along, the foresters murmured amongst themselves, for they were not happy with the King's promise

Silhouette of a Magician (Firkin, Public Domain).

to Herne to be made Head Forester. They were jealous and angry that their order of promotion would be upset and they plotted Herne's downfall. So when they arrived at the wizard's hut, they confronted and threatened him with his life if he allowed Herne to live.

"I cannot permit the King's servant to die now," the wizard answered, "but I shall predict that he will not be a forester for long." Delighted with this news, the foresters mounted their horses and made to depart. But as they were leaving, the wizard called out, "Remember this! Herne's misfortune will follow you, foolish men that you are!" Despite this warning, they laughed and spurred on their horses back to Windsor.

One month passed and Herne returned. He presented himself to the King, who was overjoyed to see him recovered. He duly appointed him the grand title of Head Forester and bestowed upon him three gifts: a purse full of gold coins; a silver hunting horn; and a golden chain which he hung round Herne's neck. And, though well pleased with these gifts, Herne was also invited to take lodgings in Royal Windsor Castle itself.

Thus, Herne began his new duties as leader of the foresters. However, all was not well. His old woodcraft skills seemed somehow to have declined and the King could no longer rely on him on the hunt. He trailed behind the hunts, was thrown off his horse, and his aim with bow and arrow was no longer true. When the other foresters became aware of this, they talked together in private, pleased at what they had observed. Finally, the King tired of fruitless hunts and said to Herne, "Loyal subject, I can no longer keep you on. So, even though it sorely grieves me, I shall have to ask you to leave." Whereupon Herne turned, jumped upon his faithful steed and, with a crazed look on his face, rode off into the forest.

Rumour spread that Herne had gone mad, which was reinforced by a sighting of him later that day. He was seen riding wildly through the forest, but this time he wore once again the antlers and he whirled his chain. No-one knew where he rode to or from. This was the last time that Herne was seen alive, for one of the foresters later came upon a gruesome sight. Whilst travelling homewards, he happened to pass a great oak tree, and noticed something which appeared to be hanging from one of its sturdy branches, and upon coming closer he discovered the body of Herne.

Terrified, he ran to the castle to fetch his fellows, but when they arrived at the tree, the body had disappeared. Although pleased at Herne's disappearance, they were also not a little disturbed at the turn of events.

That night, Herne's Oak, as it was later to be known, was blasted by lightning during a tremendous thunderstorm. From that time on, it was not unusual for the ghostly form of Herne to be seen hanging by unfortunate travellers passing by that fated tree.

An Old Oak, by James Ward (1769–1859) (Public Domain).

These ghostly occurrences did not go unnoticed by the foresters, who became very uneasy. Indeed, it now appeared that Herne's troubles had fallen upon them, for they too began to lose their skills and knowledge of the woodland and hunt. It was then they recalled the wizard's last words: "Remember, Herne's misfortune will follow you!" Fearful that they would also incur the King's displeasure, they decided to consult the wizard.

They therefore hastened to his hut, where he was busy mixing liquids and ointments. Upon hearing them arrive, he stopped his magical works and met them outside, whereupon they at once implored him to remove the curse, as they were very frightened. The wizard's answer, however, was plain. "You have brought this upon yourselves. I can help you no more, except to make one suggestion. If you wish to make amends, then go at midnight as if to hunt to the tree where Herne took his life. There you may discover what you have to do," he told them.

And so it was that at midnight the foresters, horses and dogs gathered at Herne's Oak. It was a cool, clear night with a full moon which threw an eerie light on the woodland scene. The foresters looked this way and that, but could see nothing until a form suddenly materialised to one side of the tree. There was no mistake as to who the apparition was, as the antler-bedecked figure of Herne the Hunter beckoned them to him.

"Follow!" Announced Herne in a cracked, hollow voice. Too afraid to disobey, they arranged themselves behind Herne as he mounted his phantom horse and the troupe fled into the dark night. Away they rode until the early hours, a wild hunt led by a ghostly wild huntsman. At their return, Herne stopped and cried, "Listen! You are now my hunting party. Those who refuse to join me will suffer the King's punishment! Return here at midnight tomorrow!" With that, he turned his horse and disappeared into the forest.

Thus, the foresters did as they were bidden, but at the end of each nocturnal hunt, Herne repeated his words: "Return here at midnight tomorrow!" And so, many were the tales of the wild hunt which led to rumours and fear. Some saw this as an omen of disaster and some a warning for folk to mend their sinful ways. Others blamed it for the death of their cattle or some other misfortune.

But none was more concerned than the King himself, who had got to hear of these unearthly happenings. He was also suspicious, for the stock of game was being depleted, as the deer were successfully hunted by the night riders. He therefore confronted the foresters and forced the sorry tale from them. He decided there was only one thing to do – to speak to Herne's ghost himself.

He arrived at the oak at midnight and, as before, the spectral form appeared with his band of followers. The King, nervous of seeing his former servant in such a guise, approached Herne and asked, "Why do you haunt these parts in such a terrible manner?" To which Herne replied, "Vengeance is my quest! I was driven to live a spirit life by the actions of these wretches." He pointed at the band of foresters. "If you take their lives in the way I took my own, then I shall cease haunting this forest for as long as you reign." The King looked at the foresters, who were under Herne's spell, and he agreed to the request. "So be it," replied Herne, who promptly rode off with his terrible entourage. The next morning, the King had the foresters hanged, after which he was disturbed no more by Herne's troubled spirit.

True to his promise, Herne the Hunter's wild hunt was not seen again until after the King's death. And so it has been seen to this day. Sometimes it is just a sound heard in the depths of a storm – horses' hooves, howling hounds, hunting horns, as well the rattling of chains. At other times, Herne himself is seen, antlers aloft and blowing his silver horn, his two black hounds by his side and followed by his phantom troupe. The wild hunt is said to appear at times of national crisis, when it is reported to dash through Windsor Great Park accompanied by a hideous throng and frightful cacophony. Perhaps he will never disappear for good, but what is certain to endure is the legend of Herne the Hunter.

(1) The legend of Herne the Hunter was first recorded in William Shakespeare's 1602 play, *The Merry Wives of Windsor*. The version you have just read is largely based on the novel *Windsor Castle* by the author W. Harrison Ainsworth, dating from 1843.

(2) Herne's Oak was cut down in error in 1796, during the reign of King George III. It had been highly regarded by the locals of Windsor. In 1906, King Edward VII planted Herne's Oak no.2 on the site of the original tree, where it stands to this day.

(3) Sightings of Herne the Hunter have occurred right up to modern times, the last by a soldier on guard at Windsor Castle in 1976.

(4) So, if you hear the thud of horses' hooves in the night, or the sound of a hunting horn, you may see the antlered ghost of Herne the Hunter of Windsor Forest.

The above is an unpublished story of Herne the Hunter for young folk, written by this author.